THE REAL READER'S QUARTERLY

Slightly Foxed

'Circus Tricks'

NO.53   SPRING 2017

Editors Gail Pirkis & Hazel Wood
Marketing and publicity Stephanie Allen & Jennie Paterson
Subscriptions Alarys Gibson, Anna Kirk, Olivia Wilson, Katy Thomas &
Hattie Summers

Cover illustration: Alice Pattullo, 'The Potting Shed'

Alice Pattullo lives and works in East London. She explores British traditions, folklore and superstitions in her personal work, producing limited-edition screen prints for exhibition and sale. She is currently producing work for her largest solo show to date which will open this summer at the Yorkshire Sculpture Park. She has also just produced her first children's book, *An Animal ABC*, published by Pavilion. Alongside this personal work, Alice works as a commercial illustrator. Her clients include Crabtree and Evelyn, Faber, Puffin, Sainsbury's, the National Trust and the V&A Museum. For more of her work visit www.alicepattullo.com.

Design by Octavius Murray

Layout by Andrew Evans

Colophon and tailpiece by David Eccles

Published by Slightly Foxed Limited
53 Hoxton Square
London N1 6PB

tel 020 7033 0258
fax 0870 1991245
email all@foxedquarterly.com
www.foxedquarterly.com

Slightly Foxed is published quarterly in early March, June, September and December

Annual subscription rates (4 issues)
UK and Ireland £40; Overseas £48

Single copies of this issue can be bought for £11 (UK) or £12 (Overseas)

All back issues in printed form are also available

ISBN 978-1-906562-98-4
ISSN 1742-5794

Printed and bound by Smith Settle, Yeadon, West Yorkshire

Contents

From the Editors   5

Circus Tricks · ADAM SISMAN
John le Carré, *Tinker, Tailor, Soldier, Spy*   7

A Flickering on the Staircase · MAGGIE FERGUSSON
Hilary Mantel, *Giving up the Ghost*   13

Moments of Truth · CHRISTOPHER RUSH
Leo Tolstoy, *War and Peace*   18

Dog Days · SARAH LAWSON
Albert Payson Terhune, *Lad: A Dog*   25

The Abyss Beyond the Orchard · ALEXANDRA HARRIS
The letters of William Cowper   29

Stage Lightning · ISABEL LLOYD
Brian Bates, *The Way of the Actor*   35

A Lesson in Living · ALISON LIGHT
John McGahern, *The Barracks*   41

Bloody Conquest · CHARLES ELLIOTT
Noël Mostert, *Frontiers*   46

Taking the Poet at His Word · JIM MCCUE
Editing *The Poems of T. S. Eliot*   51

Reading Maps · ROBIN BLAKE
On maps in books   55

Contents

Trouble in Ruritania · KATIE GRANT
Violet Needham, *The Black Riders*   63

Angling for a Bit of Peace · DAVID BEANLAND
Arthur Ransome, *Rod & Line*   68

Age of Innocence · ANTHONY GARDNER
Godfrey Smith, *The Business of Loving*   71

A Song of the Islands · PAMELA BEASANT
George Mackay Brown, *An Orkney Tapestry*   76

Time Out of War · JEREMY LEWIS
Robert Kee, *A Crowd Is Not Company*   81

Along the Old Ways · URSULA BUCHAN
W. H. Hudson, *A Shepherd's Life*   86

The Book Cure · KEN HAIGH
Rediscovering the love of reading   91

Bibliography   95

John Watson

For the digital edition of *Slightly Foxed* and an up-to-date list of partners
and membership benefits, please visit the members' page on our website:
www.foxedquarterly.com/members or contact Olivia:
oliviawilson@foxedquarterly.com · +44 (0) 20 7033 0258.

The Slightly Foxed office can obtain all books reviewed in this issue,
whether new or second-hand. Please contact Anna:
annakirk@foxedquarterly.com · +44 (0) 20 7033 0258.

From the Editors

Spring, and it's precisely thirteen years since the first issue of *Slightly Foxed* appeared. Then of course we had no idea of what *SF* would become – more of a friendly worldwide fellowship of readers than simply a magazine. Many of you have been with us from that first issue, and our subscription renewal rate is unusually and cheeringly high. As we frequently tell you, it's your loyalty and enthusiasm that keep us going, and this year we've decided to express our appreciation to you in a more concrete way.

If you are a subscriber you will find enclosed with this issue a personal *Slightly Foxed* membership card along with details of the benefits that go with it. These range from discounts on all things *Slightly Foxed* to reductions on membership of a number of organizations we feel are likely to appeal to readers of *SF*, such as the London Library and the Royal Society of Literature. It's a varied but carefully chosen list, and though we'll be adding to it as time goes on, we promise we'll keep it that way. If your subscription expires with this issue, you will receive a membership card as soon as you renew.

Inevitably in thirteen years the index of authors and contributors who have featured in *Slightly Foxed* has grown to epic proportions. Some of you will have received the printed updates we've provided over the years, but they're expensive to produce and inevitably go quickly out of date, whereas the interactive index on our website, www. foxedquarterly.com, is updated with every issue and is available as a download. So we've decided to give up on the printed version: do phone us on 020 7033 0258 if you have problems with downloading, and we will be happy to help or do it for you.

Many of you have been collecting our handsome reissues of Ronald Welch's Carey novels for children in the Slightly Foxed Cubs series. All twelve are now available and this Spring we're adding an interesting postscript – a thirteenth novel which is not technically part of the series but which just as well might be for it has all the same ingredients – a young protagonist with a Welsh background, a believable cast of characters, and a fast-paced plot brought alive by Welch's customarily vivid historical detail.

Sun of York is set during the later stages of the Wars of the Roses, the fearful struggle between the houses of York and Lancaster that saw the last gasp of the Middle Ages. Impoverished young aristocrat Owen Lloyd goes to war on the Yorkist side determined to fight his way to wealth and power and to take revenge on the Turberville family who have seized the Lloyds' estate. His exceptional courage and ability bring him to the notice of influential people at Court and give him an inside view of the ruthless cynicism of those struggling for power – and an unexpected view too of the character of the future king Richard III. Though disillusioned, Owen returns to Wales a wiser and more mature young man. A fascinating picture of fifteenth-century warfare and politics which fills a gap in the original series, *Sun of York* is available to order from us now at £17.50 (subscribers £16).

This Spring's new Slightly Foxed Edition, Hilary Mantel's *Giving up the Ghost* (see p. 13), is one of the most powerful memoirs we've reissued, uncompromisingly honest and written with all the brilliance we've come to expect from this extraordinary novelist. Here she is dealing with both the inner and outer truths of her own life and growing up – laying the painfully persistent ghosts that eventually drove her to forge her own remarkable path. It's a truly haunting book which we can't recommend highly enough.

And finally, many congratulations to the winner of our 8th crossword competition, Mrs E. Blackman, who receives a free annual subscription. For those still chewing their pens, the answers appear on p.95.

GAIL PIRKIS & HAZEL WOOD

Circus Tricks

ADAM SISMAN

I first read John le Carré's *Tinker, Tailor, Soldier, Spy* soon after it was published in 1974, and have reread it several times since. It is one of those books that never fails to give me pleasure, even now I know it so well. There is so much about it to admire and enjoy: the precision of the dialogue, the deftly drawn characters, the accuracy of the settings, the steadily rising tension – above all, the sheer quality of the writing. Here is a writer in complete command of his subject: able to do whatever he wants, confident it will succeed.

For me, and I expect for most readers old enough to remember it, the book has become enmeshed with the BBC adaptation, first broadcast in 1979, in which Alec Guinness played the lead role of George Smiley. Just as I have read and reread the book, I have watched this adaptation several times over, with the effect that many of the lines have become imprinted on my mind. The script echoes the novel – almost literally, in the sense that much of the dialogue is lifted unchanged from the book, though the story is told in chronological sequence, rather than as a succession of flashbacks. In fact it is a surprise not to find certain familiar lines in the book on rereading, and to realize that they derive from the television series. 'Poor George,' Smiley's wife says to him at the end. 'Life's such a puzzle to you, isn't it?' – a line which is absolutely true to the characters, and to the spirit of the book, but which derives from Arthur Hopcraft's script, not from le Carré's novel.

John le Carré, *Tinker, Tailor, Soldier, Spy*
Sceptre · Pb · 432pp · £8.99 · ISBN 9780340993767

I must confess that I hadn't noticed this until I came to write le Carré's biography. And indeed researching le Carré's life has enhanced my appreciation of his work, and of *Tinker, Tailor, Soldier, Spy* in particular. The more I discovered about the circumstances in which the novel was written, the more I came to admire his achievement. When he began it, his career was in crisis. His previous book, *The Naïve and Sentimental Lover*, an attempt to break out of spy fiction, had received a critical pounding: one critic pronounced the book 'a disastrous failure', another, 'the product of self-indulgence and intellectual laziness'. This was his third novel in succession to receive the thumbs-down from the critics. The fact that *The Naïve and Sentimental Lover* had drawn directly on his own experience made the criticism feel more personal. He had opened up his private feelings to public scrutiny, and been mocked for it. Small wonder that he was 'extremely hurt' by the book's reception. 'My hardest duty to myself was to keep the bitterness at bay,' he would later recall.

Those who have not had a book published may not appreciate how destructive reviews can be. Years of effort can be dismissed in a few glib sentences. Much of the criticism of *The Naïve and Sentimental Lover* had been *ad hominem*; it was even suggested that le Carré's career had run its course. To be denigrated in print is painful, of course; but more damaging was the threat to his self-belief. Without confidence that what one produces is worthwhile, it is difficult, if not impossible, to write. Le Carré's recovery from the drubbing he had taken would be a test of character as much as of talent.

But he remained resilient: bruised, but still standing. And he refused to succumb to resentment. His return to the espionage genre would prove to be one of his most accomplished performances to date. The new book was planned as the first in a sequence of interlinked novels. He talked of seven, or even more: perhaps as many as ten or fifteen. The overall theme would be the struggle between 'the Circus' and the KGB, in particular the contest between George Smiley and 'Karla', the mysterious and apparently all-powerful head of the 'Thirteenth Directorate of Moscow Centre'. Like the Circus, an intelligence organization roughly corresponding with MI6, the Thirteenth Directorate was an imaginary body, though Moscow Centre was real slang used by KGB agents themselves.

For le Carré, the actions of the intelligence services revealed the true, hidden nature of the state they represented. The Circus was England in miniature, looking back with nostalgia, and contemplating the future with foreboding. Smiley's generation of senior officers, now approaching retirement, had been among England's most gallant knights in the crusade against Nazism; their reward had been to see their country reduced to the status of a second-class power. 'Poor loves,' laments a drunken Connie Sachs, the Circus's discarded head of research: 'Trained to Empire, trained to rule the waves. All gone. All taken away. Bye-bye world.' She is nostalgic for a golden past, and the exploits of courageous young men; she does not want to hear that any of them might have betrayed his country. 'I want to remember you all as you were. Lovely, lovely boys.'

Taken as a whole, therefore, the sequence of novels provided an opportunity to train a light not just on the secret state but on the state itself, in its painful attempt to come to terms with its post-imperial role. This was a scheme that went far beyond the limits of the genre, on the scale of similarly ambitious projects in post-war fiction by such 'literary' writers as Paul Scott, Anthony Powell and C. P. Snow. Le Carré's inspiration was Balzac. 'I had originally intended to do an espionage *Comédie Humaine* of the Smiley-Karla stand-off, and take it all over the world,' he would tell an interviewer in 2002: 'a kind of fool's guide to the Cold War'. This of course was a throwaway comment: his real aim was to examine the state of the nation, by exposing its secret underside.

The evolution of the book through successive drafts demonstrates two of le Carré's qualities as a writer: his ability to develop and manage an exceptionally complex plot without a pre-planned scheme, and his commitment to re-work what he has written over and over again until he achieves the result he wants. '*Tinker, Tailor* was the most difficult book I ever wrote,' he would recall five years after it was published. In it he explored 'the inside-out logic' of a double-agent operation, demonstrating the mayhem that could be caused by such an agent in a position of influence within the intelligence services, as Kim Philby had been. For all the startling revelations about Philby, George Blake and other spies, few people fully understood what le Carré called 'the push-me-pull-you nature of the double agent's trade':

> For while on one side the secret traitor will be doing his damnedest to frustrate the efforts of his own service, on the other he will be building a successful career within it . . . The art of the game . . . is therefore a balancing act between what is good for the double agent in his role as loyal member of his service, and what is good for your own side in its unrelenting efforts to pervert that service, to the point where it is doing more harm to the country that employs it than good; or, as Smiley has it, where it has been pulled inside out.

It is revealed in the opening pages of the novel that there is a Soviet 'mole' at the heart of British intelligence, controlled by Karla. 'A mole is a deep penetration agent, so called because he burrows deep into the fabric of Western imperialism,' explains Irina, an unhappy Russian agent wanting to defect. The unidentified mole, code-named 'Gerald', is said to be 'a high functionary in the Circus'. This discovery presents the authorities with a dilemma. 'We can't move,' laments the Minister's advisor, Lacon:

> We can't investigate because all the instruments of enquiry are in the Circus's hands, perhaps in Gerald's. We can't watch, or listen, or open mail . . . We can't interrogate, we can't take steps to limit a particular person's access to delicate secrets. To do any of these things would be to run the risk of alarming the mole.

'It's the oldest question of all, George,' Lacon says to Smiley: 'Who can spy on the spies?' The answer is of course Smiley himself, who has been sacked in a purge following the downfall of his boss, known only as Control. Smiley is called out of retirement to lead the mole-hunt. Working in secret, with only a couple of trusted assistants, Smiley studies old files and interviews former colleagues, reconstructing the past in his mind, using his imagination to fill the gaps in the evidence. It is a scholarly sort of thriller, yet one in which menace is ever present.

One of the strengths of the book is a vivid sense of place – of the dingy hotel which becomes Smiley's centre of operations, of the third-rate prep school where the betrayed agent Jim Prideaux now teaches, above all of the Circus itself. Some of the most compelling scenes are set there. In le Carré's previous novels the Circus had been comparatively nebulous, but here it springs sharply into focus. The anonymous entrance, the garrulous janitors, the dingy interior, the warren of corridors and the clanking lifts – all create the illusion of a real place: as well they might, because the interior of the Circus is based on Broadway Buildings, the headquarters of the Secret Service in le Carré's time with MI6. He carefully reconnoitred his locations, and recorded them in photographs taken from different angles. He modelled the Circus's exterior on an unassuming building (since demolished) which, he told an American journalist, 'had some of the same qualities of dilapidation and anonymity'. His concern for

detail extended to identifying individual rooms within the imaginary set-up.

As in le Carré's previous books, the sense of authenticity is made keener by the use of jargon, some of it real, but much of it invented: 'the Cousins' (Americans), 'the Competition' (MI5), 'scalphunters' (specialists in dangerous operations), 'babysitters' (bodyguards), 'pavement artists' (agents conducting surveillance), and so on. Some of these coinages have proved so useful that they have subsequently been adopted by intelligence professionals. I like the fact that le Carré does not bother to explain such terms, but leaves the reader to work out what they mean.

Ultimately *Tinker, Tailor, Soldier, Spy* is a whodunit. There is a moment, about two-thirds of the way through, when Smiley realizes what has been going on: 'at the heart of this plot lay a device so simple that it left him genuinely elated by its symmetry'. The Circus has been 'turned inside out' by a traitor, so that its energies and its resources are working not against Karla, but for him. When at last the 'mole' is unmasked, Smiley realizes that he has always known who it was – as has everyone: 'all of them had tacitly shared that unexpressed half-knowledge which like an illness they hoped would go away if it was never owned to, never diagnosed'.

Tinker, Tailor, Soldier, Spy is one of my favourite books. I urge anyone who hasn't read it to do so immediately. You are in for a treat.

ADAM SISMAN is the author of *John le Carré: The Biography*, published by Bloomsbury. He is a Fellow of the Royal Society of Literature.

A Flickering on the Staircase

MAGGIE FERGUSSON

In 1994, Hilary Mantel joined the Council of the Royal Society of Literature, where I was working as Secretary. She was in her mid-forties, and her sinister and hilarious fourth novel, *Fludd*, had been a big hit with our President, Roy Jenkins. Her fellow Council members warmed to her immediately. Matronly, but always beautifully dressed, she combined clear thinking with a cracking sense of humour, frequently shaking with laughter at the RSL's eccentricities. So it was always a disappointment when, ahead of meetings, a note in her bold, steady hand curled out of the fax machine: she was ill, she couldn't come, she was sorry. What was the nature of this illness? In 2003 her memoir *Giving up the Ghost* was published. I took it on holiday to Scotland, and read it in one great gulp. Then I understood. Asked what triggered the book, she admits that she never intended to write a memoir, and that it came about almost by accident. The sale of a weekend cottage in Norfolk moved her to write about the death of her stepfather, and from there 'the whole story of my life began to unravel'.

It is a story that crepitates with ghosts. She lays down provisions for them, stocking her larder with more food than she and her husband could ever eat, cramming her freezer with meat and her airing cupboard with spare linen. Some of the ghosts have names. Within the first few pages we are introduced to her dead stepfather, Jack, who manifests himself as a 'flickering on the staircase'. Then there is the daughter she never had, Catriona, who is gifted at all sorts of things Hilary is not – driving, dealing with money, making curtains. Mostly, though, these 'wraiths and phantoms', which she believes flap around us all, can't be precisely identified. They creep under carpets and into the fabric of curtains, lurk in wardrobes and under drawer linings. They represent versions of ourselves that might have been. 'When the midwife says, "It's a boy", where does the girl go? When you think you're pregnant and you're not, what happens to the child that has already formed in your mind?'

Mantel has suffered more might-have-beens than most; but her childhood begins happily enough. Born into a working-class Catholic family near Manchester in 1952, she was for some years an adored only child – 'Our 'Ilary' ('my family have named me aspirationally, but aspiration doesn't stretch to the "H"'). She is brilliant at capturing a child's semi-understanding, and her early memories are pin-sharp. She sits in her pram, the trees overhead making 'a noise of urgent conversation too quick to catch'. She climbs on to the knee of her tall, thin, intelligent-looking father, Henry Thompson, 'helping' him with the crossword by holding his pen, clicking the ballpoint in and out 'so it won't go effete and lazy between clues'. She likes to be close to people who are thinking – to enter the field of their concentration. While her father reads the racing pages, she imagines the horses: 'I picture them strenuously'.

She falls in love with certain words: 'scorn', 'bastion', 'citadel', 'vaunt' and 'joust'. She dreams of becoming a Knight of the Round Table, and believes that when she is 4 she will turn into a boy. Meantime she is 'fat and happy', her composure only occasionally shaken. One day she eats a green sweet from a cheap selection called Weekend, and becomes convinced that while putting it in her mouth she has breathed in a housefly. 'There is a rasping, tickling sensation deep in my throat, which I think is the fly rubbing its hands together.' The fear of death stirs in her chest 'like a stewpot lazily bubbling'. She wonders whether to tell her parents she is dying.

School comes as a shock. None of the other girls seems interested in her bag of grey plastic knights or her knowledge of chivalric epigrams. Mantel, meanwhile, cannot understand their eagerness for a game called 'water', which consists in floating plastic ducks to and fro across a basin. Nor can she comprehend the absurd questions posed by the teacher, Mrs Simpson: 'Do you want me to hit you with this ruler?' The only possible response to such inanity is silence. '"Hilary's crying again"' the other children chant – and no wonder. One day a nun, Mother Malachy, hits her so hard on the side of her head that she is propelled across the room, her head spun round on the stalk of her neck.

Before Hilary moves on to senior school – the Convent of the Nativity, where she becomes head girl – life at home has undergone a seismic change. One afternoon a man called Jack Mantel comes for his tea, and never leaves. In sharp contrast to her father, Jack is a rowdy presence, keen on weightlifting and singing. Quiet Henry remains in the house, moving into a single room. It is as if he is melting into the walls. Her mother stops going out. Hilary, eavesdropping on adult conversation, tries to get some purchase on what is going on. She feels responsible for her father's misery – there is something in her 'beyond remedy and beyond redemption'. It is 'the worst time in my life'.

'Work out what it is you want to say,' Mantel counsels novice writers, 'and say it in the most direct and vigorous way you can.' But even for somebody of her astonishing talents, some things are almost unsayable. One afternoon, playing in the back yard, her sight is drawn to something some fifty yards away, among coarse grass, weeds and bracken. She can't exactly see anything, but she is aware of a disturbance of the air. She senses 'a lazy buzzing swirl, like flies; but it is not flies'. Though there is nothing to see, to smell or to hear, she can intuit, at the limits of her senses, the dimensions of 'the creature'. It is roughly the height of a two-year-old; it is a foot or fifteen inches deep. Something intangible has come for her – 'some formless borderless evil, that came to try to make me despair'. She is left shaking, 'rinsed by nausea'.

It is tempting to see this *Lord of the Flies* moment, which knocks for six Hilary's already shaky belief in an omnipotent God, as a manifestation of all that was wrong at home. When Hilary's mother and Jack moved house, her father stayed behind. He was never mentioned again 'except by me to me'. They never met again. But his absence did not bring happiness or peace. Everything Hilary did seemed to enrage Jack: 'I was in trouble for being a girl, for being thirteen, for being fourteen. All my behaviour seemed to anger him, just by the fact of being behaviour: but silences, absences, were also a provocation to him.' She skates over her teenage years in just a couple of pages, but there are hints of strain, and even violence. 'There was tension in the air of our house, like the unbreathing stillness between the lightning and the thunder.'

What do you do when your family falls apart? Mantel's instinct was to glue herself into a new unit. By the time she was 20 she was married to a geologist, Gerald McEwan, whom she was to divorce and remarry before she was 30. She was a student at the LSE, planning to become a lawyer and a politician. But by then there were intimations of a new kind of agony. Most people's illnesses are as dull as holiday snaps, but Mantel's descriptions of her symptoms have a gruesome fascination. From time to time something seemed to flip over and claw at her 'as if I were a woman in a folk tale, pregnant with a demon'. Pain wandered about her body, 'nibbling here, stabbing there, flitting every time I tried to put my finger on it'. The doctors dismissed her as an over-intense, over-ambitious girl, dosed her up with Valium and sent her packing. It was eight years before they accepted Mantel's self-diagnosis of endometriosis, a condition in which the cells lining the womb grow in other parts of the body, bleeding monthly and binding the internal organs together.

The diagnosis meant an immediate hysterectomy, and the onset of the menopause. 'I was twenty-seven and an old woman, all at once.' In response to hormone treatment she began to balloon. From a seven-and-a-half stone slip of a thing she swelled outward, gathering fat in 'places you never thought of'. By the age of 22 she had realized she would never have the stamina to become a lawyer or a politician, and had made a conscious decision to become a writer instead. By the time she hit 50, though still frequently unwell, she had eight novels under her belt.

Even as a successful writer of fiction Hilary Mantel felt for a long time unable to write about herself. Her life had been written by others – parents, teachers, the child she once was, and her own un-born children 'stretching out their ghost fingers to grab the pen'. All were reflecting back contradictory versions of her: a fat sylph, the mother of a 'paper baby', a chronically ill malingerer, a wife and not a wife, Mantel but really Thompson. Writing *Giving up the Ghost* is an attempt to 'seize the copyright', to take command of her memories, and so gain some distance from them. But as she reveals in a rapid-fire interview at the end of my battered paperback, it was originally intended as a purely private exercise, like her diaries, only to be read by others after her death. What made her change her mind she doesn't say; we can only be grateful that she did. In a crowded field, this is perhaps the strangest, most shocking, warmest and wittiest memoir to have been published this millennium

MAGGIE FERGUSSON is Literary Director of the Royal Society of Literature and author of *George Mackay Brown: The Life* and *Michael Morpurgo: From War Child to War Horse.*

Hilary Mantel's memoir *Giving up the Ghost* (232pp), is now available from *Slightly Foxed* in a new limited and numbered cloth-bound pocket edition of 2,000 copies (subscriber price: UK & Eire £16, Overseas £18: non-subscriber price UK & Eire £17.50, Overseas £19.50). All prices include post and packing. Copies may be ordered by post (53 Hoxton Square, London N1 6PB), by phone (020 7033 0258) or via our website www.foxedquarterly.com.

Moments of Truth

CHRISTOPHER RUSH

In a celebrated passage in Tolstoy's *War and Peace*, a girl is dancing – a young girl not yet out of her teens. She is an aristocrat, a countess from St Petersburg, and she is visiting the village home of a distant relative whom she calls her uncle. He is a jovial character who lives with a serf woman, Anisya, who has prepared a rustic banquet for the hunting party. The girl is Natasha, the heroine of Tolstoy's novel. She is filled with an ingenuous enthusiasm for life and is enchanted by this sudden slice of bucolic living, so far removed from genteel city circles. After the meal she is enchanted by the sound of the balalaika. At the introductory chord to a folk-dance, 'Uncle' genially commands her to dance it. She has never done such a thing before, but she flings off her shawl, sets her arms akimbo, makes the preparatory motion with her shoulders, and proceeds to perform the dance to perfection, to the amazement of her audience – and, it seems, of the author.

> Where, how, and when could this young countess, who had had a French *emigrée* for governess, have imbibed from the Russian air she breathed the spirit of that dance? . . . Her performance was so perfect that Anisya Fyodorovna . . . had tears in her eyes, though she laughed as she watched the slender, graceful countess, reared in silks and velvets, in another world than hers, who was yet able to understand all that was in Anisya,

The Penguin edition of Leo Tolstoy's *War and Peace* (1869), translated by Rosemary Edmonds, that Christopher Rush read is now out of print but a new translation by Richard Pevear and Larissa Volokhonsky is available from Vintage: Pb · 1,296pp · £9.99 · ISBN 9780099512240.

and in Anisya's father and mother and aunt, and in every Russian man and woman.

In another famous passage in *War and Peace* the cold and distant aide-de-camp Prince Andrey Bolkonsky lies wounded, in and out of consciousness, during the Battle of Austerlitz, having just rescued his battalion's standard. As evening advances, he gazes up at the loftiness of the sky as if he had never seen it before. Three riders approach. '*C'est une belle mort,*' says one of them, looking down on what he assumes to be the corpse of the soldier who had carried the standard. One of the others replies, addressing the first as *Sire*, and Bolkonsky understands that the man he is now looking up at is Napoleon, whom he actually reveres more than his own tsar.

> But he heard the words as he might have heard the buzzing of a fly . . . Napoleon seemed to him such a small, insignificant creature compared with what was passing now between his own soul and that lofty, limitless firmament with the clouds flying over it . . . He was only glad that people were standing near, and his only desire was that these people should help him and bring him back to life, which seemed to him so beautiful now, now that he had learned to see it differently.

He manages to move his leg and utter a groan. Napoleon immediately orders him to be given medical treatment – which saves his life.

These two scenes each produced a profound impression on me when I first sampled *War and Peace* in the 1957 Penguin edition at the age of 13. Our English master had informed the class that our households were not properly furnished unless they contained the King James Bible, the Works of Shakespeare and *War and Peace*. Two years later I read *War and Peace* properly. Hundreds of scenes impressed me, though at the time it was the two scenes I have described that produced the biggest impact. I wanted to marry

Natasha. As I couldn't, I decided I would at least marry a Russian. Eventually I did. And then BBC Radio 4's marvellous adaptation of *War and Peace* on New Year's Day 2015 prompted me to reread the novel and to marvel anew.

Each passage cited above is about life. Each describes an epiphany in which the character experiences a life truth. Natasha seizes a moment in which the genetic memory in her bursts into flower and she feels life on her pulses and in her limbs and whole body. The dance is literally in her blood. Or, putting it another way, it's an expression of her soul – the Russian soul. The wounded Andrey sees life as he never saw it before. The world is as beautiful for him as it is for Natasha and he wants to be alive in it. Peace and war are the settings, but both these scenes describe life-changing, life-affirming moments.

This is where the title of the novel is so important. The title Tolstoy finally settled on was taken from the political theorist Pierre-Joseph Proudhon's book *La Guerre et La Paix* (1861), a title which means precisely what it says and no more. But when Tolstoy completed and published the final version of his novel *Voyna i mir* in 1869, the word *mir* carried a number of connotations and meanings, including a slightly obsolete one referring to society, mankind. In this sense the word could mean, roughly speaking, humanity. Tolstoy's novel is concerned not merely with war and the cessation of war, it is about human beings, all mankind, for whom war is a vast muddle, which is the curse of society. It is about the triumph of the human spirit in time of war; and the side that wins the war is the side that displays the stronger spirit. Natasha's dance and Andrey's sudden understanding of what matters are triumphant leaps of the human spirit: each results in an inner joy, a peace.

War and Peace is written with a realism which is unprecedented in Russian literature. Tolstoy can persuade his readers of anything, irrespective of the truth or otherwise of his narrative. The truth is in the massive energy of the writing, awesome and terrifying. In the first scene just described Tolstoy is asking us to believe in genetic memory, which allows an impeccably bred and ultra-refined aristocrat – also a slip of a girl – without the necessary rustic upbringing or tuition, or even a moment's pause for reflection or rehearsal, spontaneously to perform the dance to perfection and to the astonishment and admiration of both the onlookers of her own class and the serfs from whose lives and culture she is so far removed.

We accept Natasha's dance because the author allows us no other explanation, and because it says something about ourselves and why as individuals we can transcend our circumstances and overcome history. By the end of the reign of Catherine the Great Russian society had become fractured, the nobility apeing French manners and dress, addressing each other in French, and slipping into Russian only when addressing their servants or giving way to impulse and emotion. Natasha's dance heals the fracture. As she dances, society is seamless again (this is the reverberation in Orlando Figes's choice of the title *Natasha's Dance* for his cultural history of Russia, 2002). The dance epitomizes the unquenchable Russian spirit which Tolstoy believed, rather than tactics and battles, made it possible for Russia to win the war against the French. You can work outwards from this scene to embrace the entire meaning of the novel, which is not only about survival but about how one should behave, how one should live. Writing about Maupassant Tolstoy once said that the novelist must have a clear idea about what is good and what is bad, and the moral concerns of *War and Peace*, all part of plot, people and style, are what contribute to its tremendous impact.

In the Austerlitz scene Prince Bolkonsky learns to live, to want to live, and to see what he has not seen before. He is given a glimpse of infinity, a glance at God. Easy to argue that in his weak and wounded state what he experiences is a mere trick of the brain, a near-death experience at the edge of consciousness. But the scene convinces because of the writing and its cinematic power to let you look through the eyes of the supine soldier. Later in the novel, when Bolkonsky does die after wounds received at Borodino, the epiphany is completed. This time the hero-worshipper of Napoleon, again seeing his hero face to face and now actually facing death, has learned a truth which deprives him of words when Napoleon asks him how he is feeling: 'Gazing into Napoleon's eyes, Prince Andrey mused on the unimportance of greatness, the unimportance of life, which no one could understand, and the still greater unimportance of death, the meaning of which no one alive could understand or explain.'

Wilfred Owen once famously wrote that he 'saw God through mud', the mud-cracked faces of the Great War trenches.

> War brought more glory to their eyes than blood,
> And gave their laughs more glee than shakes a child.

The troubled characters of Tolstoy's novel, troubled because they are essentially good people, have found glory and laughter in the end, arising out of war. They have found peace.

*

It was in 1862, the year of the fiftieth anniversary of the pivotal Battle of Borodino, that Tolstoy discovered the key to the final form his novel would take – in Victor Hugo's five-volume *Les Misérables*. Here he found the epic digressiveness and the lyrical, historical and political mix that would give his own work its unique character and transcend the novelistic genre. To Hugo, Napoleon represented the highest expression of the human spirit, whereas Tolstoy saw him as the lowest. He simply couldn't bring himself to believe that an arrogant upstart such as Napoleon could control the destinies of nations, and he convinced himself instead that the higher a man rises in the chain of command, the less depends on him or on his will. Opposed to Napoleon is Kutuzov, the pacifist and fatalist, who believes that things will follow their predestined course. Tolstoy portrays him as humble and unaffected, free from Napoleon's massive vanity.

By the time *War and Peace* was written, Tolstoy's beliefs had crystallized into a philosophy of fatalism under Providence. We see a similar situation in the *Iliad*, where the destinies of men and nations are already decided, and, despite all the struggles of individuals and armies, events will unfold according to Olympus. Reading *War and Peace* with its many complex strata of life and interwoven stories of aristocratic

Tolstoy at work shortly before his death in 1910

families, you can see Tolstoy working out his view of men as rather like ants or bees, crawling about the surface of the earth, and here there is another parallel with Homer's cosmic eye and the view taken by gods both merciless and benign.

Tolstoy himself said of *War and Peace* that it was not a novel, even less a poem, and still less a historical chronicle. His aim was to teach by boldly blurring the lines between history and fiction in order to get closer to the truth. He realized, like Plato, that literature is more philosophical than history and therefore more true, even as it departs from mere fact. It was Tolstoy, furthermore, who brought a new kind of consciousness to the novel, with his godlike ability to hover over and within actions and characters, his cinematic use of detail, and the techniques of panning, wide shots, close-ups and aerial artistry, in dramatizing battles or ballrooms. In fact these devices are as old as Homer – take away his hexameters and you find startlingly novelistic and modern techniques.

There is something Homeric, too, in the freshness and vigour of Tolstoy's symbols drawn from the natural world. But they go beyond Homer's epic similes in their many-sidedness and completeness. A remarkable example is the massive and ancient oak tree seen by Prince Andrey when he is visiting his son's estate, and is weary of life. As he looks at the oak he sees an image of himself, gnarled and scarred and grim, spurning the spring sunlight, an image of hopelessness. But one night soon afterwards he overhears Natasha talking excitedly. She is thrilled by the beauty of the moon and wants to fly up into the sky; and when he looks at the oak a little later, on a return visit, it is transfigured. 'There was nothing to be seen now of knotted fingers and scars, of old doubts and sorrows. Through the rough, century-old bark, even where there were no twigs, leaves had sprouted, so juicy, so young, that it was hard to believe the aged veteran had borne them.' The veteran is a metaphor, and Andrey is now in love with the young girl who wanted to fly into the sky.

Homer's gods exult in the spectacle of mass slaughter; there is a scene in the *Iliad* in which Zeus settles down to watch a battle as a man would a football match between his two favourite teams. Tolstoy as omniscient narrator of battles is godlike, and there is no gainsaying his full-on descriptions of the carnage. Unlike Homer, however, he states his own position unambiguously through Prince Andrey: 'War is not a polite recreation but the vilest thing in life, and we ought to understand that and not play at war. Our attitude towards the fearful necessity of war ought to be stern and serious . . . Its aim and end is murder.'

Tolstoy's god looks down and does not approve, while Tolstoy himself suggests that mankind is a failed project of the universe, prefiguring by half a century the shattering of faith that came in the wake of the two World Wars. He believed that one can't live in the world as it is, it has got to be changed, so in spite of its patriotism and its religious acceptance and all else, *War and Peace* is a revolutionary novel.

CHRISTOPHER RUSH has been writing for over 30 years. His books include *To Travel Hopefully* and *Hellfire and Herring*, and *Will*, a novel about Shakespeare. His latest novel, *Penelope's Web*, was published in 2015.

Dog Days

SARAH LAWSON

If the subjects of our early reading determine what we become, I should long since have turned into a collie. As a child in the 1950s I read one book after another by Albert Payson Terhune about the pure-bred sable collies (the Lassie type) he kept on his New Jersey estate, Sunnybank. The books were published in the 1920s but even now most of them are still in print.

By the time I finished them, I had decided to become a vet. It would be gratifying to say that I stuck to this ambition and am now a retired vet, but I didn't. Nevertheless, for a few years I was keenly interested in everything about dogs and could easily imagine myself grown up and breeding them when I wasn't curing their illnesses. We had a lovable, affectionate collie at the time, and she must have blended in with her Sunnybank cousins in my imagination.

I was just one of the many readers who've fallen under the spell of Terhune's idyllic Sunnybank and its immortal collies. The 'yarns', as Terhune called them, were never written as children's stories and usually appeared first in such magazines as the *Saturday Evening Post* and *Ladies' Home Journal*, but children were always among Terhune's most devoted readers.

Albert Payson Terhune (1872–1942) was a literary writer *manqué*. In 1894, while waiting for an editorial job at Scribner's, he joined the staff of the *New York Evening World* – temporarily, he thought, but he was still there twenty years later. Eventually he decided to leave the

Albert Payson Terhune, *Lad: A Dog* (1919)
Wildside Press · Pb · 248pp · £9.99 · ISBN 9781434440495

paper, move permanently to the family's country home in New Jersey, and make his living from freelance writing. He wrote at the speed of a Dickens or a Trollope, working for eight or nine hours a day, six days a week, and producing short stories, novels and travel adventures, all the while lamenting that he didn't have the leisure to write serious literature.

Terhune had long wanted to write a dog story, but editors repeatedly assured him that nobody was interested in stories about animals, even after the success of Jack London's *The Call of the Wild* in 1903. When an editor suggested that he write 'something spicy', Terhune wittily asked if he could write about a cinnamon bear. At length in 1915 he managed to persuade the editor of *Red Book Magazine* to let him write about a dog, and he produced a somewhat fictionalized tale about a favourite collie named Lad. The story was so popular that he wrote several more adventures of the collie, and E. P. Dutton eventually published them in 1919 as *Lad: A Dog*. This collection amounts to an episodic novel. We follow Lad's exploits in the prime of his life, but at length he grows old and is nearly killed by younger dogs wishing to unseat the alpha male of 'The Place', as Sunnybank is always called.

Lad had an acute, almost human intelligence. Some readers wondered if a dog could possibly perform the feats Terhune ascribed to his collies, but he maintained that he never described a dog doing something that he had not seen his dogs do – or at any rate heard of a dog somewhere doing.

Besides being big and brave, the Terhune collie, as exemplified by Lad, is male, loyal and protective. He is a four-footed Sir Galahad. He respects children and the females of most species. He learns the Law and is obedient to the letter. Typically he begins as a boisterous puppy and then matures into dignity and heroism. Reading a biography of Terhune, you notice that, by an interesting coincidence, he too was a mischievous boy who matured into the Master, worshipped by his collies.

Terhune was a hefty six foot three and had been a serious boxer and fencer in his youth. The dogs, similarly, are skilled fighters, always looking for better bite holds, in contrast to breeds that merely clamp on to one place and then hang on for the duration. A collie's way of fighting and slashing with its teeth derives from its wolf ancestry, which Terhune assures us was relatively recent. The stories are full of such didactic little asides, some more convincing than others.

Lad is described in a way that is almost Homeric. We frequently read of his 'absurdly small' forepaws; his coat is 'mahogany'; he stretches 'fore and aft, in true collie fashion'. He weighs eighty pounds and is immensely strong, having 'mighty shoulders'. The house and grounds of the Sunnybank estate are described in detail – the veranda, the kennels, the music room, the fireplace and the dog-friendly rug in front of it. Outside is the 'fire-blue' Pompton Lake. No wonder sightseers came in droves to see the setting of these enchanting stories.

A few episodes in *Lad: A Dog* feature the buffoonish but villainous Hamilcar Q. Glure, a satirical figure on a par with some of Sinclair Lewis's creations. Glure, otherwise known as the Wall Street Farmer, tries to fix a dog show so that his own expensive, imported collie will win it. The Master and the Mistress are morose about the coming defeat of their beloved Lad, but through a comical turn of events Lad wins it after all. Glure, taking his collie through some shepherding manoeuvres, drops his lit cigar on his hand and makes many gestures unknown to the dog, who then patiently waits for an explanation before responding to any further signals.

Terhune never quite falls into the trap of anthropomorphizing his canine heroes, although he does endow them with an almost human courage and loyalty. Still, dogs can have those attributes, and canine emotions may overlap with human ones. The Sunnybank collies always remain dogs. When the omniscient narrator describes a dog's train of thought, it is always limited to the perceptions a real dog would have, and described with the insight of a man who had observed canine behaviour for much of his life. Why is Lad rolling about on a man's jacket? How does he know that the man at a neighbouring farm is the same one he chased up a tree two weeks before?

After *Lad: A Dog* appeared, readers begged for more stories about the magnificent collie. *Further Adventures of Lad* followed in 1922, then in 1929 (eleven years after the death of the hero) *Lad of Sunnybank*. Unable to visit the living dog, tourists came – and still come – from far and wide to see his grave, while clippings from Lad's coat are preserved in the Library of Congress.

By 1937 Terhune and his dog yarns were sufficiently familiar for *The New Yorker* to run a cartoon in a series called 'Literary Renegades' which pictured a tail-wagging collie, a remonstrating Master, and in the distance a woman clinging to a galloping horse. The caption read 'The Albert Payson Terhune Collie Who Failed to Stop a Runaway'.

Now demolished, the house at Sunnybank with its much-described veranda and music room stood for barely a hundred years, but readers of the books continue to imagine it at the end of the drive with the fire-blue Pompton Lake a furlong beyond, surrounded by the forests of the Ramapo Mountains. Whatever the encroachments of highways and suburbia, The Place and its collies will always be there, indestructible in a million imaginations.

SARAH LAWSON writes poetry (*All the Tea in China*), fiction (*The Bohemian Pirate*), and translations (Christine de Pisan's *Treasure of the City of Ladies*) and lives in London without a dog. Her last pet was Sweeney, an outstanding hamster.

Anna Trench

The Abyss Beyond the Orchard

ALEXANDRA HARRIS

For about a hundred and thirty years after his death in 1800, William Cowper was one of those figures about whom every keen reader had something to say. He was up there with Milton and Johnson, though people felt more intimately connected with Cowper than they were ever likely to feel with Milton. His long poem *The Task* (1785) seemed to articulate all the longed-for goodness of familiar, homely things; it was a tribute to 'Domestic Happiness, thou only bliss of paradise that has survived the fall!' Yet here, and in hundreds of the letters that began to be published from 1804 onwards, things of joy were surrounded by gulfs of loss and desolation.

Anne Brontë remembered the silent tears she wept during her childhood reading of Cowper. She cried with him, and for him, and with a sense of recognition: 'The language of my inmost heart', she wrote, 'I traced in every line.' Jane Austen defined her heroines partly by showing us the spirit in which they read Cowper: Marianne Dashwood cannot bear to hear Edward's calm rehearsal of 'those beautiful lines which have so frequently driven me wild', though it's clear that her passionate enthusiasm may not be the only way of appreciating them.

Many young readers in the nineteenth and early twentieth century worked out what they felt about life in relation to Cowper, but you'd be hard pressed to find an 18-year-old driven wild by him today. Millions now read Austen and the Brontës, but they stop short of the poet and letter-writer who was so important to those novelists.

We can try to obtain second-hand copies of William Cowper, *The Centenary Letters*, ed. Simon Malpas (2000).

Discovering the letters for the first time, four years ago, at the ripe age of 31, I felt the full force of a literary revelation. Why had no one urged them on me before? The book I had in my hand as I sat in a blue cane chair at the end of the garden (I remember it vividly, as you do when you read things that matter) was a small collection of the letters, edited very helpfully and lucidly by the Romantic scholar Simon Malpas.

The prose struck me immediately as gloriously elastic. Long sentences unfurl themselves, clause after clause, stretching an arm here and there to pull in some extra detail surely not planned at the outset and yet effortlessly incorporated into a perfectly grammatical and balanced whole. Effortless: was it? I couldn't tell. I paused over sentences like this one, in which Cowper ponders – with such apparently spontaneous extravagance – the gap between his own generation and his forefathers'. We look back, he says, 'almost upon creatures of another species':

> Their vast rambling mansions, spacious halls, and painted casements, the gothic porch smothered with honeysuckles, their little gardens and high walls, their box-edgings, balls of holly, and yew-tree statues, are become so entirely unfashionable now, that we can hardly believe it possible, that a people who resembled us so little in their taste, should resemble us in any thing else.

He was expatiating, in fact, on the difference between his own writing and that of a century or half-century before, when prose – like topiary – was clipped into shape. Cowper's heel-kicking, free-reeling elegance, by contrast, felt modern. It reminded me of Virginia

Yew-Tree Statues

Daniel Macklin

Woolf's letters. Then I realized that of course she had read the eighteenth-century letter-writers as a girl, when her own prose style was forming. She borrowed Cowper's letters from her father's library (and went back, she remembered, eager for the next volume). These, then, were rhythms she knew well. I read on.

I felt I was listening, as much as reading, since the writing had the qualities of talk. This was certainly what Cowper aimed for: his highest ambition for a letter was that it should be like conversation. He wanted intimacy and spontaneity. He wanted both the rapidity and the luxurious lengthiness of relaxed exchange between friends. Writing to Joseph Hill one morning in December 1781, he imagined it to be late afternoon, his favourite time in winter, when the fire could be lit. Such convenient adjustments were a letter-writer's prerogative. 'I will suppose it afternoon, that you and I dined together, are comfortably situated by a good fire, and just entering on a sociable conversation. You speak first, because I am a man of few words.' He proceeded with a dialogue, which is of course an uninterrupted monologue. Cowper, a man of many words, as well as wide learning and political interests, wrote on through the morning, despairing of the continued war in America, recommending withdrawal, but seeing this defeat as the ruin of England.

Cowper often wanted to discuss politics and he wanted to discuss religion (which he saved for his evangelical correspondents, knowing how others tired of it). But many of his epistolary friendships were founded on a desire to talk, with sympathetic people, about not very much at all. He reasoned that since friends often talk just for the pleasure of being in each other's company, letter-writers are quite justified in doing the same. 'A letter may be written upon any thing or nothing just as that any thing or nothing happens to occur.'

Cowper had a gift for writing about nothing, which was fortunate, since nothing happened often to occur in the course of the quiet life he lived in the Buckinghamshire market town of Olney. This was how he liked it, or rather this was how he needed things to be. Since leaving London in the throes of a suicidal breakdown in his early thirties, he had lived as quietly as he could, dependent on the kindness of friends, keeping up the routines of walking, writing and gardening that helped to soothe his hourly dread of damnation.

While he did 'nothing', while he tended his cucumbers, for example, he was often in excruciating mental pain. He appreciated his surroundings intensely, but complete happiness was impossible because he believed himself to be shut out from God's love. He had no business with pleasurable things, though they might be lent to him for brief enjoyment. Coming in from his greenhouse in May 1780 he said to himself what he was always saying, 'This is not mine, it is a plaything lent me for the present; I must leave it soon.' This is the desperate fact that lies behind even his most delightful letters. To write about oysters was to fend off the devil for an hour.

His correspondents could not always keep up. 'When I write to you, you answer me in fish,' he chided one friend on receipt of mackerel and lobster. What good was fish as a letter? Nevertheless: 'though they never spoke in their lives' (the mackerel and lobster, that is) 'and it was still less to be expected from them that they should speak, being dead, they gave us an assurance of your affection.' Often he wrote in extended anticipation – for example of a visit from his beloved cousin Harriet Hesketh. For months in advance of her proposed arrival he would lay out the scenes that would meet her. For months afterwards he would recall them to her. Rarely can a single modest house and a few square miles of English countryside have been so feelingly described.

Astonishingly, it's all still there. Olney is on the A509 between

Northampton and Milton Keynes. The traffic races past, but Cowper's house, Orchardside, is stopped in time, its sash windows facing on to the market place. It is now the Cowper and Newton Museum – the Newton being John Newton, the evangelical curate and abolitionist who first brought Cowper to Olney and with whom he wrote the *Olney Hymns*.

There were only two other visitors to the museum on the afternoon I went there with my friend Felicity James, a Romanticist who had long ago understood the line of intimate connection from Coleridge's conversation poems back to Cowper's talkative writing. Our reading paths had crossed at Cowper; and when we looked on the map to find a meeting-point between her home in Leicester and mine in Oxford, Olney was the place we found.

The house looks large from the street, but it's unaccountably dark and cramped inside. Tripping over a wooden hutch in the hall – could it really be one of the hutches Cowper made himself for his pet hares? – we understood that this wasn't a pastoral idyll. In this rather unhomely-feeling house, we saw why Cowper valued each item of crockery and piece of furniture. Here they all were, straight out of the poems and letters, each simply labelled: 'Cowper's Moveable Bookshelves', 'Cowper's Coffee Pot', 'Cowper's Lavender Water'. As we arrived upstairs to find 'Cowper's Razor' (once owned by John Betjeman, who reread *The Task* each year) and a lovingly reproduced pair of 'Cowper's Stockings', we could hardly believe the completeness with which a personal world had been reassembled.

Here, among these things, Cowper talked on and on, imagining his correspondent across the room. In the huge Oxford edition of the *Letters*, edited by James King and Charles Ryscamp, the conjuring from nothing goes on through five volumes. It's oddly gripping. After several hours you look up and find that all you have to report to an enquiring friend is that Lady Hesketh, having postponed her visit to Olney so repeatedly that it seemed doubtful she had any intention of coming, has at last sent her bedstead on ahead of her, but the bedstead, so Cowper reports, has not arrived at Orchardside and is deemed lost.

For the lengthy pursuit of beds (this one turns up at the inn), for the twists and turns of Cowper's mental agonies, for the development of his political thinking, and for the week-by-week commentary on his progress in the translation of Homer, one needs the Oxford volumes. Never before have I spent so much on a set of books, but these I wanted by my bed, since Cowper is hard to read in libraries. In libraries one wants to be getting on with things, making a great many notes before the bell rings, whereas Cowper (who in fact kept his working hours punctiliously) requires that you put the notebook away and read as if there were no pressure of time at all.

What's so finely judged about Simon Malpas's selection is that it honours the expansiveness of the letters, their supernumerary arabesques and reiterations, while also pressing on through the years. There are the mackerels and the coffee pots, and there are the nights of screaming in terror. 'I am hunted by spiritual hounds in the night season,' Cowper told William Hayley, unable to keep up a pretence of cheerfulness. Through the 1790s he was hounded beyond all comfort and security. Pleasure was now, he wrote, 'a faint recollection'. The scenes he once loved were powerless to soothe him. Looking up from my blue cane chair on that summer day four years ago, I thought this little volume of Cowper's letters was perhaps the saddest book I had ever read. Leafing back through its pages of courtesies and cameos, books and fish, political justice and religious madness, fond jokes and sentimental gifts, I realized how strenuously Cowper's artful talk was holding back the real nothing: the abyss that he saw, day by day, just beyond the orchard.

ALEXANDRA HARRIS is the author of *Romantic Moderns* and *Weatherland*, which she adapted in ten parts for BBC Radio 4. She is Professor of English at the University of Liverpool. Having started out as a modernist, she is currently reading her way around the eighteenth century.

Stage Lightning

ISABEL LLOYD

In 1987, I was at drama school in Cardiff: by the sea, and all at sea. A swotty, wannabe rebel who'd done well at university, I'd swerved into a one-year acting course where closely argued, thesis-synthesis intellectual habits were useless. More than useless. They were, the gimlet-eyed improvisation teacher said as I gurned and stuttered through her class, *a problem*.

Thank goodness, then, for Brian Bates. I can't remember which teacher told us to read his new book, *The Way of the Actor* (1986). But I can remember the sense of relief when I realized that, despite the icky subtitle – *A New Path to Personal Knowledge and Power* – it was written by a professor of psychology and had footnotes; this I understood.

Bates's ideas were intriguing. Using his own interviews with four leading actors – Charlton Heston, Glenda Jackson, Anthony Sher and Liv Ullmann – and excerpts from hundreds of other performers' interviews and memoirs, he laid out a theory that actors were shamans for the modern world. They were, he said, men and women in touch with their many subconscious selves, what older societies would have called the spirits. More, at a time when it was common currency to be snobbish about actors – they were frivolous, possibly neurotic and, in the male of the species, certainly unmanly – Bates argued that they played a vital role. They acted, literally, as lightning rods to carry and defuse society's repressed needs and desires.

The book delved at some length into why it is necessary for actors

---

We can try to obtain second-hand copies of Brian Bates, *The Way of the Actor: A New Path to Personal Knowledge and Power* (1986).

to be outsiders, how charisma is created and perceived, and the ways in which great performers can make huge spaces shrink and seem intimate. But Bates seemed particularly intrigued by the idea of extreme manifestations in performance, when actors become so absorbed in the characters they are playing that they either physically transform in some way, or have out-of-body experiences. In the rushes of *The French Lieutenant's Woman*, Meryl Streep's eyes, apparently, change colour from her own grey to the Woman's deep green; William Hurt reports watching himself perform on stage as if he was sitting at the back of the stalls.

Bates is a persuasive writer. At the end of the two nights it took to read the book, I had decided: I was going to be not just an actor, but an actor-as-shaman. In classes, in rehearsals and on stage, I tried very hard to access my inner others, to allow characters to take over and perhaps transform me. It never happened. Stubbornly, my self refused to be anything other than itself. I began to feel Bates had sold me a pup; the path to knowledge and power was actually a cul-de-sac.

After a few years stuttering through work as an actress as I had once stuttered through class, I stopped. Eventually I landed a job on the arts desk of a national newspaper, theatre took a back seat, and *The Way of the Actor* stayed, forgotten, on my bookshelf.

*

Today, I am a journalist who likes to write about actors, and Brian Bates is sort of retired. He lives with his son and grandchildren in East Sussex, where he is working on a screenplay of his first book, *The Way of Wyrd*, along with a self-help book he's co-authoring with his good friend John Cleese. We agree to meet in a café at the foot of the defunct West Pier in Brighton. Drinking coffee on a windy terrace, with long white hair blowing into his pale, excitable blue eyes, dressed in a kaftan-like patterned shirt and with large silver rings on his fingers, he looks like nothing so much as an amiable, slightly portly Gandalf.

The 1960s was the decade that discovered Tolkien, and Bates might have been conjured up as the perfect product of those unbounded, fantastical years. Brought up in the dull suburbs of England's Midlands, at 17 he was taken by his family to live in San Francisco. He's unwilling to discuss his exact age ('With all the afflictions I've had lately, I've put that aside'), but it seems he was studying psychology at the University of California at Berkeley just as the hippy movement came into its full, kaleidoscopic flowering. Not, I imagine, co-incidentally, it was also when the late American anthropologist Carlos Castaneda began writing his influential and uncertainly factual 'Don Juan' books, which claimed to describe drug-enhanced, out-of-body experiences among the tribal shamans of Mexican Yaqui Indians.

After perhaps ten years in the US, Bates returned to England to do post-doctoral research at Cambridge, before joining the psychology department of the then new – and determinedly counter-cultural – University of Sussex. He made enough of a splash, teaching courses in unusual states of consciousness, to become Chair of Psychology, but he was bored by all the paperwork, and in the mid-1970s he switched to teaching the psychology of acting to students at the Royal Academy of Dramatic Art (RADA) in London.

While he was there, he wrote *The Way of Wyrd* (1983), which he called – perhaps mindful of the ragging Castaneda received from a sceptical press – 'a work of documentary fiction'. It described an encounter between a Christian scribe and an Anglo-Saxon pagan in sixth-century Britain, and became something of a cult hit. By the mid-1980s, when Bates had spent almost a decade teaching and directing at RADA, *The Way of the Actor* must have seemed, to his publisher, a natural call.

Rereading *The Way of the Actor* now, Bates's writing seems, for a professor, surprisingly mass-market. He has a liking for the punchy, one-sentence paragraph, and no fear of marketing: in early chapters his better-thyself mantra about the path to personal knowledge and power makes regular appearances. (I'm still unclear what form that personal power might take; when I ask him in person, he says he hoped the book would encourage people 'to feel more free about exploring their selves', which doesn't entirely help.) He likes to end a chapter with a question, which he promises to answer overleaf, a journalistic trick that herds the reader onwards. But the material from the four interviews he did himself is illuminating, partly because he is exploring as a psychologist the nature of an actor's experience, and partly, I suspect, because actors are rarely interviewed about anything more challenging than what it was like being in their most recent film, and who they're sleeping with. You sense how much Sher, Jackson et al. appreciated the seriousness of Bates's questions, his forensic examination of the fine detail of their craft and the precise nature of their experiences on stage.

And Bates clearly loves actors. Discussing them on the page he's intense and serious; discussing them in person he's gossipy and animated. When I ask which of the actors at RADA were most open to his ideas of transformation and altered states, he cites a list that includes Ralph Fiennes, Timothy Spall, Mark Rylance and Sean Bean. Bates wants to tell me about an improvisation class on fairy-tales with Bean at RADA, in which a young Jane Horrocks played a princess. Princess Jane was allowed to choose a horse: 'I want Sean!' Then, according to Bates, she 'rode him about the classroom, slashing at things with her sword, before dismounting and going into a deep sleep. Sean was such a noble, gentle horse. He paced towards her on his hooves, then reached down – you could almost see his long neck stretch out, and his velvety muzzle – and he kissed her . . .' Bates's eyes sparkle at the memory. 'She squealed!' he says.

We discuss Mark Rylance – a favourite student – and specifically Rylance's interest in ritual and his belief that we are surrounded by spirits. And we talk at some length about Glenda Jackson, whom Bates interviewed when she was at the height of her fame, some years before she turned her back on theatre, slamming a bushel over the blazing light of her talent and choosing instead to become a determined, if unremarkable, politician. Bates hasn't heard the news that after a twenty-four-year absence she is acting on stage again, playing the title role in *King Lear* at the Old Vic; when I tell him, he's delighted she's back. I've read plenty of interviews with Jackson over the years where she has blocked any attempt to get to the bottom of why she stopped acting. Bates, though, in his two long meetings with her, one in her dressing-room, one over dinner, recorded this in his chapter on the risks actors take with their own sanity:

> Glenda Jackson, talking to me about the actor's relationship with the audience, characterizes it as a situation soaked with fear. 'You risk the whole of yourself – I mean, you do actually take your life in your hands and walk out there to see if that ravening beast is going to snatch it from you or allow you to keep it for a little bit longer. Actors commit so much to the work – it is *so* important to them, that acting always puts you in a life or death situation.'

Earlier, she tells him 'the longer you do [acting], the harder it gets, because all you ever really learn are the difficulties of it'. It's easily the best explication I've seen of the fears that drove her to politics: after dealing with the beast in the stalls, Parliament must have seemed a safe option.

As the morning slips past, Bates, by increments, starts to interview me. Why do I do what I do? Why write about actors, rather than be an actor? I tell him how fascinated I was by the idea of transformation, but that I was always too analytical to get lost in a character. I say how much I enjoy watching actors and thinking about the fine detail of what it is they're doing. Much like his book did. As we chat, I realize *The Way of the Actor* may not have helped me much with acting, but it did help me write. It put me, I say, on my path to personal knowledge and power. He's delighted by this as, it seems, he is delighted by most things. He kisses me on both cheeks, and leaves, twinkling, to spend the rest of the day with his grandchildren.

*

Did he sell me a pup? Can great actors transform? Bates used footnotes; this is mine.

London, 2010. The Apollo Theatre. It's the final few minutes of *Jerusalem*, a play that has made its lead actor, Mark Rylance, a star. Rylance's character – Rooster Byron, an impish figure who claims to have met the great god Pan when walking to Bristol along the M4, and whose home and whole way of life are under threat – is beating faster and faster on a tom-tom, calling out the names of the old gods, in a last desperate attempt to put the modern world on hold.

As the tempo of the drum reaches its crescendo, Rylance flings his arms up into the air, throws back his head and whoops. He's a slight man, but his whole body swells, inflating to two or three times its normal size. His hair sticks out; his face lengthens and contorts, his eyes become huge, round and almost entirely white, like a roughly painted tribal mask. He is terrifying, unreal. Transformed.

Blackout. The house lights come up. The audience sits, silent, bathed in the sudden yellow glare. Then there is a whoosh, an outpouring of breath, and a convulsion upwards. Everyone stands on their feet, roaring and clapping and cheering. I am standing with them, but I'm not cheering. I'm thinking, over and over: 'Brian Bates. Brian Bates. *He was right.*'

ISABEL LLOYD is the international culture editor for *Newsweek*. She lives in London, and tries to stay permanently in character.

A Lesson in Living

ALISON LIGHT

Was any novelist – or journalist come to that – writing about breast cancer in the early 1960s? Did anyone – apart from the medical profession and a few bold souls – even talk about it? When I was growing up, the word 'breast' was usually only encountered in literature or hymns and was likely to summon a snigger; women and girls had 'chests'. A mastectomy was considered almost a matter of shame. Astonishing, then, that John McGahern's first novel, *The Barracks*, published in 1963, has Elizabeth Reegan's breast cancer at its centre.

My own brush with the disease is comparatively recent so for me the subject is rather close to the bone. When I came across a second-hand copy of the novel on holiday in Ireland I might have put it back on the shelf, but the blurb only mentions an 'illness' and the title suggests a wider canvas. The cover of the 1980s Faber paperback shows two men in garda uniform lounging outside a police barracks, a regulation bicycle just in sight. Was this choice of image intended to attract a male readership? Not entirely, I think.

Elizabeth is married to a police sergeant and is bringing up his children in their quarters in the barracks. The pattern of their days, shared with the other gardai and their wives in a close-knit Irish village, is a counterpoint to her inner life. Her illness often puts her at one remove from people she knows intimately, their stories and their everyday dramas. Like the writer himself, she is a sympathetic but also a critical observer. And so *The Barracks* is a novel about how

---

We can try to obtain second-hand copies of John McGahern, *The Barracks* (1963).

to live and what matters in a life; the way we all feel part of things and yet, so often, are alone and disconnected. Elizabeth's illness is a kind of crucible for McGahern, intensifying and clarifying what matters to him.

Breast cancer used to be thought of – and often was – a sentence of death. A sense of awful inevitability hangs over the novel, and the stages of Elizabeth's disease – diagnosis, hospital treatment, recuperation – form the time-frame of the book. But the forward march of chronology is halted in its tracks by moments of reprieve or remission, when Elizabeth sees the beauty of the world and feels at peace. One of the achievements of the book is its pace: a slowing down and savouring of experience.

The Reegans and their neighbours live a bare existence, cultivating allotments because they cannot even afford vegetables for their families, and struggling to find the money for doctors' bills (there is no NHS). McGahern speaks from inside these lives without condescension or self-consciousness. His often rather formal prose elevates the ordinary almost to a sacred plane – the right type of rain to fish by, the soaking of bacon in warm water when it is too salty, a circle of white frost under the shade of a sycamore tree. The novel celebrates the small rituals which, like those of religion, can offer 'calm and grace and reassurance'. Elizabeth derives sustenance from the daily drawing down of the blinds, putting tea on the table, or warming her husband's clothes in front of the fire before he comes in from his rounds. These are the creative acts of everyday life which are quietly precious.

McGahern spent much of his own young life in a police barracks where his father was indeed a sergeant, and an authoritarian. Though his novel is affectionately humorous and steeped in the language of the rural community, there is never any sentimental 'Oirishry' or what the novelist Anne Enright recently called 'Paddywhackery' about it. McGahern knows that routines also cramp and stifle us; that the same funny story, endlessly retold by a neighbour, soon becomes banal. Elizabeth's husband John is eaten up with anger and resentment. One of the generation of idealistic young men who fought for the Irish Free State and hoped it would give them better lives, he finds himself lorded over by a censorious and despotic Superintendent whose petty diktats echo the conservative Irish society of the time. John and his fellows have little to do. They write fictional patrol reports and spend most of their time grubbing an existence from the land. Reegan's desperate need for money to free himself from the police makes him exploit his children, bullying them in turn and warping their lives.

McGahern is always breathtakingly truthful about other human beings. Having lost one wife, John's first private reaction to Elizabeth's illness is utterly believable: 'How could two wives die on the same man? It was incredible.' Yet this selfish, surly man is capable of tenderness. One of the most touching scenes is that of middle-aged lovemaking between the couple – another taboo broken, perhaps – where familiarity, comfort and warmth are every bit as important and uniting as passion. 'It didn't have to mean anything more than that, it'd be sufficient for this night.'

The Barracks is not 'sick lit.' There are few physical details. We follow Elizabeth through her disbelief and terror, and her rage and despair, but we also see her enjoyment of hospital where responsibility slips from her and she has the rare treat of being looked after. Coping with the reactions of other people exhausts her. In one darkly comic scene her well-meaning but nosy women neighbours want all the details of her disease and stay all hours, 'holding back the dogs of their egos till they could unleash them to the sweet indulgence of their own unique complaint'. (Anyone who has been laid up will recognize this.) Yet we never lose sight of the loneliness and weariness of their lives. Elizabeth herself is petty and tyrannical and far from noble. Sometimes she finds the idea that life will go on after her death horrifying; in a different mood, it provides solace. She realizes she would have asked the same questions as she got older in any case:

'What matters in a life? Does life have a purpose?' At best she is simply happy to acknowledge that 'she was just passing through'.

I love the seriousness of this novel and its meditative quality. *The Barracks* is ultimately concerned with humility, with the getting of wisdom. For Elizabeth the basis of a spiritual life means embracing the world rather than rejecting it or looking to the next (unlike the patronizing priest who urges her to join the local 'Legion of Mary' and is furious when she resists his probing of her faith). McGahern is sceptical, though, about Ireland's future if it becomes a purely individualist, secular society where 'getting on in the world' is all that matters. The local doctor remarks to Elizabeth that Irish society post-war is now freer and less class-ridden. 'The pig-in-the-kitchen days are gone,' he tells her, boasting that he can now enter a swanky hotel in Dublin without apology or trepidation. Elizabeth is impressed by his conviction but asks herself, 'What difference could being able to walk proudly into the Shelbourne Hotel possibly make in any real person's life?'

McGahern became better known in Britain when he was shortlisted for the Booker Prize in 1990 for *Amongst Women*, another nuanced account of female lives under the sway of male authority. Was *The Barracks* a book before its time? When it was reprinted as a Faber First in 2009, the cover carried a photograph of a woman peeling potatoes into a colander. Would author and editor give the novel a different title now, more in keeping with the central character? But what else could it be called? The barracks is a place of regulation and confinement, of generosity and of kindness – like the village and the home – places where differences between people can be weapons or a source of delight. We all struggle against the deformation of our lives by power or money or ego, trying to live with others and yet be ourselves.

I've come to John McGahern's novels crabwise, scuttling sideways. Ten years ago I read his gentle, Proustian *Memoir*, which treats of his childhood and his mother's death, also from breast cancer. I can see now that *The Barracks* was an extraordinary leap of imagination for a young man, putting us in the woman's position. But it is more than that. Like Tolstoy's Ivan Ilych facing his death, Elizabeth's narrow, local life takes on the force of a universal truth. Like her, we don't know when we will die, only that we will. *The Barracks* made me weep but it also filled me with wonder. I found the novel consoling and enriching, for it is founded on a sense of mystery, a word the author returns to, alive to those moments of grace and joy in the everyday world, and to the 'ecstatic' power of remembrance which protects us against violence and stupidity, and the capacity we all have for destructiveness. Separate and sometimes sealed off in our individual consciousnesses, still the need for union and connection returns and gives us the peace which for Elizabeth resolves into 'the one desire to love and to cause no living thing pain'. These themes reach their consummate expression in McGahern's final great work, *That They May Face the Rising Sun*, written nearly forty years later. But *The Barracks* is just as full of humanity and compassion.

ALISON LIGHT's latest book, *Common People*, used her family history to follow the lives of the itinerant working poor. Like many English people, she has Irish ancestors but doesn't think she will get very far with only 'Murphy from Ireland' to go on.

Bloody Conquest

CHARLES ELLIOTT

There is a temptation to approach Noël Mostert's *Frontiers* (1993) circumspectly, as you would the Grand Canyon or the Great Pyramid of Giza. It's monumental – 1,292 pages, not counting index and notes – and frankly imposing, a doorstopper to stop the largest door. The story it tells is of vast proportions too. Do not, however, be unnerved. This is a book which for originality, historical depth and sheer narrative richness has been compared to Gibbon – and it deserves the comparison. It also deserves a great many readers.

Do those last sentences sound like something extracted from the jacket copy? Maybe a bit hyped? They might, because as editor of the book I wrote the jacket copy for it in the first place. But I wouldn't want to give the impression that I praised *Frontiers* then only in order to sell it, and that I am now inclined to back away. On the contrary. Having spent a couple of weeks reading it all the way through again, my admiration for what Mostert achieved is greater than ever.

Frontiers started out as a much smaller book, intended to deal primarily with one of the most shocking and tragic episodes of the nineteenth century, the mass starvation and death of the Xhosa people. The Xhosa, South Africa's most populous and sophisticated group, had made the terrible mistake of listening to the teachings of native prophets and in consequence committed a sort of national suicide. In researching these mysterious events, however, it soon became apparent to Mostert that to do justice to his subject he would

---

We can try to obtain second-hand copies of Noël Mostert, *Frontiers: The Epic of South Africa's Creation and the Tragedy of the Xhosa People* (1993).

need to move back in time. His idea of what the book should be grew and grew, stretching further and further back into South African history and even prehistory.

I don't mind admitting that, as his editor, this expansion of the project made me nervous – I had signed *Frontiers* on the strength of his earlier splendid (but normal-sized) book *Supership* and hadn't bargained for a monster. Mostert, I know, was unsettled too. Still, one thing I have learned in a career of shepherding books into existence is that you probably shouldn't challenge either the author's conception of a book or the degree of detail he chooses to bring into it, providing he knows what he wants and is in control. Mostert, clearly, knew what he wanted and was in control of his material. The resulting book is nothing less than a full-scale account of the collision between two worlds, white European and black African, over the course of centuries.

It is a wonderfully complicated tale including everything from set-piece battles to moving evocations of life in the deserts and forests before the coming of settlers, from the quiet heroism of a few missionaries like James Read to the bombast of an important colonial bureaucrat like Sir Harry Smith, in Mostert's words 'one of the most extraordinary personalities of all, dashing, vain, self-glorifying, reckless, somewhat mad, and often ludicrous, as well as silly'. And along with the exceptional characters come many small visions that stick in the mind: a trekboer family moving in an ox-drawn wagon across the flat, empty Karoo with all their belongings and animals, at the pace of the slowest – the chickens; or dead bodies in the aftermath of an attack, with their insides neatly scooped out by vultures, leaving only dry skin and skeletons. There is nothing bloodless about Mostert.

Some reviewers of *Frontiers*, dazed by its length, claimed that the first two or three hundred pages could have been omitted. I can see their point, but I wouldn't go along with it. These chapters cover the long period from the first arrival of Bantu-speaking blacks in South Africa up to the minuscule colony of Dutchmen starving on the meat of penguins beneath the shadow of Table Mountain. There is wonderful stuff here, about the Age of Exploration, about the nature of the aboriginal cultures that occupied the land before the white invaders, about the first bemused contacts between blacks and shipwrecked Europeans. Nothing, in fact, is really superfluous: in the wild independence of the rural Dutch Boers we see the inevitable pressure for more land, and the seeds of apartheid; in the initial mild resistance of the Xhosa the beginning agony of their destruction.

The British took over the Cape from the Dutch in 1797 for purely strategic reasons. Curiously, given the wars that would be fought over it – no less than eight, progressively more violent, over the course of a century – nobody much wanted it. (Even Nelson couldn't see any point in possessing the place.) It indeed soon proved itself a nuisance. For the British government the colony was a constant drain on the Exchequer, with a seemingly endless series of elderly Waterloo veterans sent out as governors who constantly demanded more troops. For the troops themselves, absurdly arrayed in full battle kit including scarlet coats and pipe-clay straps even while struggling through the stifling bush, South Africa offered little but discomfort or worse. As for the settlers shipped out from England to occupy seized territory, their lot was fear – fear of the climate, of the wildlife and especially of the natives, whose deeply loved homeland was being stolen.

Frontiers succeeds brilliantly in showing how the interwoven forces – the increasingly disaffected Boers, the settlers, the colonial administration, the distant London government, the missionaries – shaped the events of nineteenth-century South Africa and led to doom for the original inhabitants. Some, particularly the Khoikhoi (pastoral nomads once called Hottentots), the first to fall, became virtual slaves to white farmers or conscript fighters. The Xhosa, on the other hand, clung to their ancestral traditions and their lands, but to less and less avail. Lied to, betrayed in broken treaties, they were gradually forced to yield land and turn to bitterness. It is difficult to argue with Mostert's sad sympathy for them. The colonial government, nearly always in the hands of British military men, had no strategy but repeated clumsy assaults by troops untrained for bush warfare. Such attacks, when they failed – as they usually did – frequently degenerated into a policy of scorched earth, leaving expanses of burnt kraals and ravaged fields. The Xhosa fought back when they could, at first with shields and assegais, eventually with muskets.

It took many years and many casualties for the British to learn guerrilla warfare. Instead there were ventures like the typically mismanaged one, splendidly described by Mostert, that took place in 1851 in the heart of Xhosa country when the British tried to clear warriors from a rugged mountain valley called the Waterkloof. Week after week ill-equipped soldiers struggled up and down the undergrowth-choked ravines of what they called Mount Misery in desperate heat, seldom finding their quarry and instead suffering constant ambush. Meanwhile, in fatuous dispatches, the British commanders were claiming victory.

Ultimately, of course, the Xhosa didn't have a chance. Pleas to London had eventually brought the colonial government more regular troops, providing Governor Sir Harry Smith with an opportunity for a more effective campaign. Though he had once remarked that 'humanity shudders' at the tactics he chose to use, he then embarked on a deliberate 'starving-out system'. This had been, as Mostert notes, 'the strategy of desperation' in every war since 1812. And in this case, it worked. By 1856 'the frontier Xhosa were in a severe state of spiritual, political and economic crisis . . . A heavy fatalism had settled upon them . . .' Their most cherished lands were gone; they were economically up against the wall.

At this point the story reaches its terrible climax. In some of the book's finest and most affecting writing, Mostert describes how the strange predictions of an unlikely prophet, a young girl named Nongqawuse, merged with current events and the deepest Xhosa traditions to create a lethal new gospel. Cattle were already dying from a lung disease accidentally introduced from Europe; there were rumours that the Russians – since they were already fighting the British in the Crimea – might come to the Xhosa's aid. Word spread that the Xhosa's long agony could end and the lost lands be restored, if only everyone took several painful steps: all the cattle – the principal source of Xhosa wealth – had to be killed; standing grain and all stored food be destroyed; and all sowing and cultivation be stopped. Then, on a certain morning, signalled by two suns rising, so-called 'new people' would rise from the sea in a grand resurrection and drive the British out of South Africa for good. Nearly all the Xhosa obeyed, however reluctantly. 'From this commitment,' Mostert writes, 'there began to unfold what is probably the greatest self-inflicted immolation of a people in all history, the saddest and most overwhelming of all South Africa's many human tragedies.'

For a time, joy and eager anticipation reigned among the Believers, convinced that deliverance was at hand. But as each appointed date came and went, month after month, doubt spread. At first, failure was blamed on the sceptics who refused to kill their cattle. By the end of 1856, however, it was inescapably plain that the prophecy was wrong. The Xhosa were left with nothing but dead cattle and empty storage bins; overfed vultures circled overhead. 'The stench of a feast had become that of a famine.' Estimates of the dead ranged up to 40,000, with thousands more driven west into Cape Colony in search of work, only to die there.

Some Xhosa survived. But the entire tribal structure was shattered, never to recover. Most of the chiefs ended in chains, imprisoned on Robben Island, a century later the place where Nelson Mandela, himself a Xhosa, would be held. The pain and anger lived on, to play a shaping role in the troubles besetting South Africa even today. For bringing us an understanding of this, if nothing else, *Frontiers* deserves its epic scale.

CHARLES ELLIOTT is an American editor and the author of several (much smaller) books.

Taking the Poet at His Word

JIM MCCUE

When T. S. Eliot summed up his life's work in 1963, two years before he died, it was in a *Collected Poems* of fewer than 250 pages. But when Christopher Ricks and I published *The Poems of T. S. Eliot* in 2015, the two volumes ran to some two thousand. Where did the other 1,750 pages come from? What is this new edition, and what does it mean to 'edit' poetry anyway?

When we began, eight or nine years ago, our first task was to gather the verse not in the *Collected Poems*. We did not know how much we would find (no one had ever compiled an inventory), but in the end our contents pages listed a couple of hundred additional items. Eliot had published many poems he didn't consider part of his serious work, such as *Old Possum's Book of Practical Cats* (which has perhaps made him more famous than ever before, thanks to the musical adaptation, *Cats*), and there are some he suppressed, as well as others from school and Harvard.

Those were known to specialists, but there were new finds too, such as a parody of surrealism, verses on gardening, and love poems written in his seventies for his second wife, Valerie – including my favourite, in which he rearranged the lines of William Blake's poem 'The Clod & the Pebble' so as to reverse its meaning. The respective first verses begin:

The Poems of T. S. Eliot (2015) · ed. Christopher Ricks and Jim McCue
Faber & Faber: Vol. 1 · Hb · 1,344pp · £40 · ISBN 9780571238705;
Vol. 2 · Hb · 688pp · £40 · ISBN 9780571238712

T. S. Eliot in his office at Faber [& Gwyer, in those days] during the 1920s

Blake: "Love seeketh not Itself to please,
        "Nor for itself hath any care,
        "But for another gives its ease,
        "And builds a Heaven in Hell's despair."

Eliot: "Love seeketh not Itself to please,
        But feareth it give no delight
        Dreadeth another's loss of ease
        And builds a Hell in Heaven's despite."

Eliot wrote poems for friends – on his fear of cows, for instance – or to celebrate events at the publishers Faber & Faber, where he worked for forty years, such as Walter de la Mare's seventy-fifth birthday, Geoffrey Faber's knighthood or the arrival of a black cat as the firm's 'Commissionaire'. Some were printed in rare, private editions or in obscure journals, and a couple were engraved on glass.

Fortunately, his genius was recognized early on, and from a young age Eliot's family and friends kept his letters and papers, which we studied in archives in London, Cambridge, New York, Boston, Yale and elsewhere. His work remains keenly sought after, and dealers and auctioneers generously put us in touch also with private collectors who own manuscripts and proofs. We weren't immune to the lure of the bookshops ourselves, buying multiple editions and other material.

By recording the variations between the published poems and the thousands of pages of drafts, we were able to document the processes of composition. Sometimes, the kernel of a work of genius looks reassuringly banal – a thought that might occur to any of us – but to trace its transformation is to see the art. In retrospect, we have the advantage of knowing how the poem 'should' read, but the author was groping forwards, having to invent and evaluate each tiny change. Why was he dissatisfied? Was the rewriting an improvement? Very often, when an alternative is presented, you can see how it is better, but you also see that you'd never have imagined how much needed changing – or how little.

In writing 'Little Gidding', Eliot typed a dozen drafts and discussed their precise phrasing in exchanges with his friend John Hayward. We document all the changes and the comments, line by line. In another instance, Eliot drained the life out of a poem as he fussed over it (a heartfelt complaint about the commercialization of Christmas became a Nobel prize-winner's official communiqué about the joy of the Second Coming) – so as well as the published poem, we printed the earliest drafts in full in our Textual History. The author's judgement stands, but comparison is invited.

All this attention to drafts and printings was part of our primary duty as editors, to establish a reliable text. For instance, in all previous editions, two of Eliot's most famous poems each have a line missing, which we have restored. In *The Hollow Men*, a line went astray at the foot of a page in 1925 and no one noticed, and in *The Waste Land* Eliot deleted a line at the request of his first wife – but afterwards reinstated it in manuscript on at least three occasions.

Yet gathering, correcting and documenting the poems is only half the work of an edition of this kind. Since Eliot's first book was published in 1917, thousands of reviews, critical studies and biographies of him have been written. Drawing upon these, our thousand-page Commentary gives the known facts about each poem – while avoiding interpretation. Sometimes, though, a critical reading emerges from the notes. Poetry groups might, for instance, like to read the poem 'Mr Apollinax' and then read the notes, which show unmistakably that it was a fiercely polite attack on Bertrand Russell.

All literature is nourished by previous books, and the Commentary explores, in Christopher Ricks's words, 'where the poems came from and where they went to'. Using Eliot's own writing extensively, but also the books he read (and occasionally annotated), we trace the vocabulary, mythology, folklore and philosophical ideas that animated his mind. This means not only listing allusions and sources (from nursery rhymes to Dostoevsky), but also turning over the soil in which the poems are rooted: the culture of the age and the experience of the man. The *Daily Telegraph* called it 'a textual reconstruction of T. S. Eliot's brain'.

Editing is about facts and tact, about presenting things clearly while solving innumerable small editorial problems. Ever since 1922, *The Waste Land* has had line numbering, and putting back the missing line threatened to disrupt this. We solved this one – signalling that the line both does and doesn't belong – by numbering it 137a.

JIM MCCUE is a freelance editor and speaker.

The illustration sent out with a press release in the 1950s for the
'Commissionaire cat' poem, 'Cat Morgan Introduces Himself'

Reading Maps

ROBIN BLAKE

Last year the Bodleian Library paid £55,000 for a fold-out map torn from a copy of *The Fellowship of the Ring* and scribbled over by J. R. R. Tolkien. Maps, said one of the Bodleian curators, were central to Tolkien's storytelling and he had annotated this one to guide the illustrator Pauline Baynes, who was making a poster map of Middle Earth (see *SF* no. 41). I was delighted that it had landed safely in a public collection. In my opinion a good map always enhances a good book, especially when the author and a skilled illustrator have worked on it together.

I formed this opinion early in life. When I was 10 I read *Friday's Tunnel*, the first of John Verney's witty and exciting (and marvellously self-illustrated) stories about the Callendar family. On page one the 12-year-old narrator February Callendar boldly reworks the first sentence of *Alice in Wonderland*, in which Alice trenchantly states the necessity in a story for pictures and conversation. February's version insists on a third essential element. 'I intend this to be the kind of book *I* like to read, which means one with a map and drawings and talk on every page.' Yes! I thought. This is going to be the kind of book I like to read too.

The first map I ever saw in a book was at the even tenderer age of 4, when I opened *Winnie-the-Pooh* and found on the endpapers a panoptic view – an Owl's-eye view and a deliciously privileged view – of the whole of the Hundred Acre Wood. It showed every principal tree (most being individual characters' houses), the 'Trap for Heffalumps', 'Where the Woozle Wasn't' and all the other key places.

In 1931, five years after his success with *Pooh*, Shepard was commissioned to illustrate *The Wind in the Willows* and his endpapers again provided a soaring overview of the story's world: Toad Hall with its lawns running down to the river, the Wild Wood, Pan Island, the houses of Badger and Ratty, and the discreet site of Mole End, with its skittle alley and forecourt lined with plaster statues of 'Garibaldi, the infant Samuel, Queen Victoria, and other heroes of modern Italy'. There had been three previous illustrators of Kenneth Grahame's book since its first publication in 1908, but none had attempted such a picture. Shepard's now seems indispensable.

It may seem a stretch to say that play-world picture maps resemble those medieval images of earthly creation, of which the best known is Hereford Cathedral's *Mappa Mundi*. Yet these are also eye-view illustrations, though it is God's and not a bird's eye that does the viewing. Hereford's circular map, with Jerusalem at its centre, has over a thousand illustrations of buildings, ships, beasts, monsters and other real or imaginary parts and inhabitants. In fiction there are many maps of this type, mostly of fantasy worlds like Middle Earth, Oz, the Seven Kingdoms, Earthsea, Narnia and a hundred others. L. Frank Baum's original map of Oz is diagrammatic rather than pictorial, yet it is very like a *Mappa Mundi* in that it shows four colour-coded territories to the North, South, East and West, all bounded by an impenetrable desert, and with the Emerald City, like Jerusalem, occupying the exact radial centre. At least eighteen further maps of Oz, both ramifications and expansions of Baum's, appeared as the franchise flourished after the author's death, making Oz a fascinating case study in fictional cartography.

The map of a fictional mythology can

always be checked by its author. A more slippery problem is posed by actual mythology, where nothing is stable and no one can authenticate the topography. Even the ancient Greek geographer Strabo doubted whether it was possible to draw a map for the *Odyssey*. 'You will find the scene of Odysseus's wanderings when you find the cobbler who sewed up the bag of winds,' he wrote. Yet many stabs have been made at charting the course of the hero's voyage, one of the most successful being in the endpapers of T. E. Lawrence's prose translation. This shows the round Homeric world with 'Regions of Night' to the north, 'Regions of Day' to the south, and a version of the Mediterranean Sea in between. The outline of Greece is entirely recognizable, as are the Nile Delta, Cyprus and Crete.

But this is not Mercator's projection. It is a *Mappa Mundi* of the imagination with, at its centre, a 'sea so vast and dread that not even in a twelvemonth could a bird hope to wing its way out', as Lawrence's

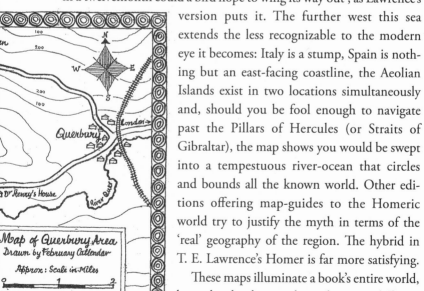

From John Verney's *Friday's Tunnel*

version puts it. The further west this sea extends the less recognizable to the modern eye it becomes: Italy is a stump, Spain is nothing but an east-facing coastline, the Aeolian Islands exist in two locations simultaneously and, should you be fool enough to navigate past the Pillars of Hercules (or Straits of Gibraltar), the map shows you would be swept into a tempestuous river-ocean that circles and bounds all the known world. Other editions offering map-guides to the Homeric world try to justify the myth in terms of the 'real' geography of the region. The hybrid in T. E. Lawrence's Homer is far more satisfying.

These maps illuminate a book's entire world, but other book-maps have the quite different function of providing a hinge for the plot. They are usually more diagrammatic – perhaps of an escape route, the streets of a dubious town or the plan of a haunted house – and what they convey, above all, is the spirit of adventure. T. E. Lawrence was himself a trained military map-maker and he provided his *Seven Pillars of Wisdom* with beautiful coloured cartography 'adapted from War Office material as embodied in GSGS 2957', which well serves the book's double identity as both a military history and a glorified boy's adventure story.

The prototype of the late-Victorian juvenile adventure genre, devoured by boys of Lawrence's generation, is R. L. Stevenson's *Treasure Island*, published in 1883. A map is so important in this that, after an extended prelude at the Admiral Benbow Inn, the action only really starts as Dr Livesey breaks the seals of the package found in the dead pirate's sea chest and 'there fell out the map of an island, with latitude and longitude, soundings, names of hills, bays and inlets, and every particular to bring a ship to a safe anchorage'. The chart, which Stevenson made sure was printed beside the text, is of a kind known as a portolan – a navigational chart – but what sets the imagination tingling, for characters and reader alike, are the 'several additions of a later date . . . above all, three crosses of red ink – two on the north part of the island, one in the south-west, and, beside this last . . . these words: "Bulk of treasure here".'

Not many adventure stories are as famous as *Treasure Island* but a rival appeared only a year later: H. Rider Haggard's colonial veld-buster *King Solomon's Mines*. The rivalry was admitted. Haggard had bet a friend that he could turn out a land-based story every bit as successful as Stevenson's sea saga, and he pulled it off with a plot, written at

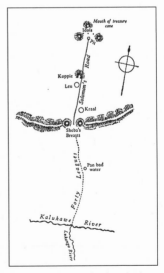

Rider Haggard's map of Kukuanaland from the first, 1884 edition

incredible speed, that similarly turns on the existence of a secret map. This is a crude land map whose primacy Haggard's first publisher stressed by providing a 'facsimile' in a fold-out frontispiece. It is coloured in rusty red on white, since the map was drawn (we are told) in a desert cave using the last drops of the mapmaker's own blood. He wanted, as he lay dying, to point the way across the African veld to 'Kukuanaland' where, as the map's inscription says, 'with my own eyes I have seen the countless diamonds stored in Solomon's treasure chamber'. To get there, the white hunter Allan Quatermain must find two hills which the map labels (enticingly for its boy readers) 'Sheba's Breasts'. He must then 'climb the snow of Sheba's left breast till he reaches the nipple, on the north side of which is the great road Solomon made, from whence three days' journey to the King's Palace'.

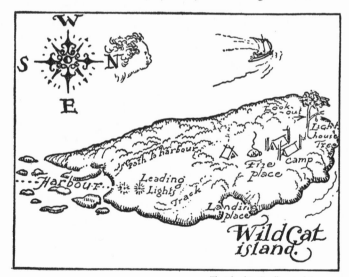

The island in *Swallows and Amazons*

Most of Arthur Ransome's 'Swallows and Amazons' books are founded in stories of the Stevenson-Haggard type, being about pirates, gold mining, seafaring and exploration. Their originality lay in showing 'real' children acting the adventures out as elaborate holiday games to which the world of adults is substantially – but never completely – subordinated. Ransome's endpaper maps underline this lineage back to the adventure stories that he had read as a boy, and he published no book without them. He also occasionally incorporated more detailed maps among the illustrations: the island in *Swallows and Amazons* itself; the area around Beckfoot with the ruined building in which Dorothea and Dick hide out in *The Picts and the Martyrs*; and the paths taken up the glen by the Decoys and Red Herrings in *Great Northern?* to divert the egg collector from the rare birds' nest. Ransome's interest in maps peaked with *Secret Water*, the plot of which revolves entirely around the holiday task set for the Walker children by their father – to make maps while 'marooned' on an island somewhere in a muddy Essex estuary. As a besotted 9-year-old my eyes dwelled again and again on Ransome's maps. If I catch sight of one now, a whole year of my childhood reading flashes past my mind's eye with a Proustian jolt.

Maps may be common in fantasy and historical novels, and not unusual in children's stories and detective fiction, but literary fiction rarely has them. I have seen editions of Virginia Woolf's *Mrs Dalloway* with useful plans of the protagonists' movements around London, and of *Tarka the Otter* with maps of Exmoor and 'the two rivers', though the latter appeared only after the book landed on the children's bookshelf, having originally been published as an adult title. I have seen, too, an illustrated map of Proust's Paris, but only in the endpapers of Stéphane Heuet's extraordinary and Tintinesque graphic version of *À La Recherche du temps perdu*. Another novel series, Trollope's Barchester stories, boasts a charming hand-drawn map of Barsetshire, with Plumstead Episcopi, Gatherum Castle and other significant places marked, but this appears only in the Penguin Classics de luxe edition. There is surely scope for more of the kind. Why not a route map of Humbert Humbert's flight with Lolita across America, or a map of Jay Gatsby's Long Island, or of Cranford, Middlemarch, Blandings Castle, Gormenghast?

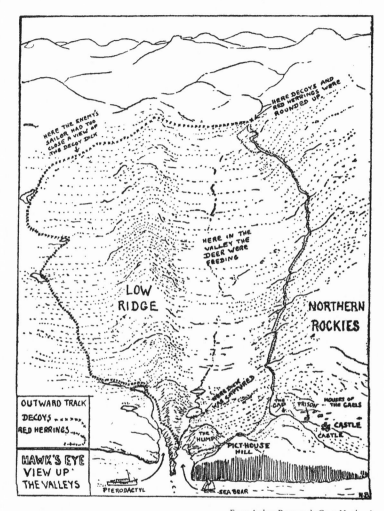

From Arthur Ransome's *Great Northern?*

If there is one heavyweight literary novel that cries out for an integral map it is James Joyce's *Ulysses*, showing the streets and squares of Dublin as they were in 1904 – ideally reprinted from the street plan in *Thom's Official Directory* that Joyce kept continually before him as he wrote the book in far-away Trieste. Vladimir Nabokov, when teaching the novel at Cornell, would insist that his students 'had to know the map of Dublin. I believe in stressing the detail; the general ideas can take care of themselves.' Yet of more than thirty different post-copyright editions of *Ulysses* only one that I am aware of (an Oxford World's Classic) prints a map to help the reader with the rides and perambulations of Stephen Dedalus and Bloom. This may even be a reproduction from *Thom's*, though unfortunately it appears too small to identify any but the most obvious of the book's locations. Luckily, in this regard, help is at hand. There exists a magnificent atlas of *Ulysses* by Ian Gunn and Clive Hart, *James Joyce's Dublin*, which has maps of various scopes and scales, and which even gives an axiometric plan showing the whole interior of 7 Eccles Street, the marital home of Leopold and Molly Bloom.

From a literary point of view, a map in a novel is never just a set of instructions, as for getting to Kukuanaland or finding your way from the Shire to Mount Doom. It is more like a kind of reverse ekphrasis – the expression of a written text in graphic form, marked up with names and descriptions ('Eeyore's Gloomy Place', 'Here Be Dragons') and sometimes with figures and landscape details. Unlike preparing for a real journey, then, it makes little sense to consult such a map before reading the book. Its purpose is to be there for you as you go along, and it may then be looked over again when the book is finished, because a literary map offers a different and quite satisfying way to revisit a book. Even if you haven't looked at *Winnie-the-Pooh* for years, I guarantee a few moments of instant pleasure should you flip open the cover and have a good read of '100 Aker Wood Drawn by me Mr Shepard Helpd'.

All of ROBIN BLAKE's mystery stories featuring Titus Cragg and Luke Fidelis contain maps of eighteenth-century Preston and the surrounding country.

Trouble in Ruritania

KATIE GRANT

Some days, the longing to re-experience childhood is so strong I imagine it might actually happen. My longing is not whimsical nostalgia: childhood happiness was shot through with anxiety about upsetting nanny, my father or God. So while sometimes I would like to be a child again, my real longing is to re-experience first readings of now familiar books. I'd willingly trade a week of old age to recapture first encounters with Heathcliff, Mr Rochester, Mary Poppins, Ken McLaughlin and Flicka; first glimpses of Narnia, Gormenghast and Malory Towers. I'd trade more than an hour to open, with no fore-knowledge, *The Once and Future King*. I'd trade nothing, though, to re-experience the delight of discovering Violet Needham's *The Black Riders* (1939). No need. The delight has never left me.

The first in Violet Needham's Ruritanian, or Stormy Petrel, sequence, *The Black Riders* is set in a fictional Central European empire. Though I'd never been to Austria, I imagined it to be similar; friendlier and tidier than my bleak familiar Lancashire moors. Where we had dishevelled farmyards, derelict gates and rusting baths as water troughs, in 'the Empire' farms were cosy, gates swung briskly and baths were found indoors. It was discouraging to realize that though I longed to be wild as Emily Brontë's Catherine Earnshaw, I was actually more like Needham's Antoinette, Countess of Valsarnia, alias Wych Hazel, whose nerves undermine her best conspiratorial intentions. I didn't like the discovery, but I kept reading.

The Black Riders of the title form part of the imperial army.

We can try to obtain copies of Violet Needham, *The Black Riders* (1939).

'Magnificent men they were,' Needham writes, 'in black uniforms, riding magnificent black horses; not a speck of colour anywhere about them, black tunics and breeches, black saddle-cloths and bridles, black astrakhan busbies with black aigrettes; only the steel of bit and stirrup shone like silver.' Magnificence and threat are a potent mix and, though that's the longest mention they get, the Black Riders stalk the reader just as they stalk the novel's young hero. Twelve-year-old Dick Fauconbois is drawn into a rebel confederation whose cause, unfashionably, isn't democracy in the empire, only better imperial government. Not politics but conflicted loyalties are centre-stage here. Dick's father, now dead, was a Black Rider. Dick longs to follow in his footsteps yet before the first chapter is out, the Black Riders are Dick's enemies.

His new father figure, the marvellously named confederate leader Far Away Moses, so-called because 'when my enemies look for me I am always far away', is a quieter kind of influence. Under his gentle tutelage, Dick exchanges the freedom of ordinary life for life undercover, delivering vital messages between confederates, his methods of travel – on foot, by train, barge, fast car, sledge, caravan and even skates – pitching the reader between the pre- and post-industrial worlds.

Cliffhangers abound: can Dick, nicknamed Stormy Petrel by the secret police, survive the sword-thrusts through the brushwood under which he is hidden? Can he burn the confederates' papers in time? Has he given too much away to Nicholas the Shepherd? Will lovely Wych Hazel crack under pressure? Can Judith, the feisty little daughter of the ruthless, charming and unimpeachable Count Jasper the Terrible, save Far Away Moses from the firing squad?

But the plot, for all its masterly pace and excitement, is the least of it. We neither know nor care much about the ideology that drives Far Away Moses. Instead the novel taps into the perennial childish fear of not measuring up. When Far Away tells Dick that 'before the end' he will have to do things that will 'sear your spirit, not your flesh', I was terrified, not that Dick would die, but that he would let his friends down. Coming, as I do, from a family whose ancestors sacrificed all to uphold what they considered the 'one, true religion', this fear felt personal. Faced with abjuring my faith, I was pretty sure I'd be found wanting. I dreaded this failure for Dick.

And it's not quite what happens: it's worse for being more tangled. After some vicissitudes, Dick, now Count Jasper's prisoner, is offered a bargain. In exchange for the confederates' names, Jasper will free Far Away Moses from the life imprisonment which is, for Far Away, worse than death. Dick's response haunted me for years: 'Can one do one's country a good service by betraying one's friends and going back on one's word of honour?' As if that wasn't drama enough, by this time I was secretly in love with Count Jasper. Only later did I realize that in this I was at one with the author.

In my imagination, and perhaps in Violet Needham's, Count Jasper looked like a young Omar Sharif and had a similar effect. We weren't alone. The novelist and poet Michèle Roberts, like me brought up a Catholic, describes how the book 'both turned me on and made me feel guilty. Secret pleasure reading it; secret guilt.' Perhaps that's part of the novel's enduring appeal: the older you is reminded not only of being tucked up on the sofa, book glued to hands, but also of early disconcerting stirrings in hitherto unexplored parts of the body. A late developer, I think my stirrings were only in my head. Though the masculine glamour of Count Jasper invaded my dreams, I was actually mostly with Dick, learning the meaning of loyalty 'with bitter knowledge'.

Violet Needham was 63 in 1939 when this, her first book, was published, a time when the gender stereotypes of dominant men and fluttery women were still perfectly acceptable. Since my own family was hobbled by male primogeniture, the stereotypes were familiar and, so I thought then, unchallengeable. Years later, I should have come to regard the whole Ruritanian series as a historical relic: distinguished but outdated. Yet dismissal was impossible. Needham's mindset might be dated – Dick thinks nothing of taking a baby squirrel from its nest or catching moths – but what a storyteller she was!

Eschewing comic-book heroes and villains, she paints, with perfect perspective and in clear language, a muddled, emotionally complicated world into which any child of any time or place might imagine him or herself. Like us, Dick is not impossibly brave: he cries and makes mistakes. Wych Hazel's feelings for Count Jasper mirror those of Michèle Roberts – secret pleasure and secret guilt. Both Count Jasper and Count St Silvain (Far Away Moses's real name) are honourable men facing the consequences of troubling decisions. Gender roles in *The Black Riders* might be problematic to modern editors but the novel's dilemmas endure.

And Needham has much to teach modern writers about neither over-egging the pudding nor describing for description's sake. 'Perfect obedience,' Far Away Moses replies softly to 'no one in particular' when, after professing total obedience to confederate orders, Dick questions being sent to bed. Dick goes very red and runs out of the room. Needham says nothing more. Behaviour is allowed to speak for itself. With the same economy, the 'scented gloom of the pine forests', the 'great chestnut woods' and the 'broad plain, golden with harvest and cut with the silver ribbon of the mighty river' serve to make doubly dreadful the prospect of civil war's killing fields; Dick's grey and steadfast eyes connect him to his dead father; and the grand gloom of the Citadel from which Count Jasper conducts state business contrasts with the chintz curtains and gay wallpaper of the nursery at Souvenir, the grand house the Count shares with his daughter. No words are wasted.

Sometimes Needham's grown-up voice intervenes, as in Dick's 'poor little head', but these moments are few. More often, the author shares her shivery delight in ciphers, codes, notebooks and map tracings; the nervous romance of wrapping reports in oiled silks and secreting them under a jacket; the boredom of waiting and the terror of muddling a secretly agreed exchange of words. Along with Dick, I copied maps on tracing paper, thrilling to its flimsy crackle under my pencil, before folding the tracings into notebooks. Where Dick had Far Away and, eventually, a graceful bay mare called Sweetbriar, I had my dog and a stocky piebald gelding called Mischief.

Best of all, there's a word which, once heard, always means *The Black Riders*. The word is, of course, the confederates' password: 'fortitude'. Those three syllables struck readers' hearts very particularly at the time of the book's publication and continue to strike readers' hearts today. We all know what fortitude means. We all know its worth. Even now I never hear the word or use it without also hearing Far Away saying, 'Should you be walking in the street, and a passer-by bend down and whisper "fortitude", you must leave whatever you are doing and do as the speaker bids you.' As yet, nobody has ever whispered 'fortitude' to me, but I'm always waiting and just hoping I'll be up to my task.

KATIE GRANT, author, columnist and Royal Literary Fund Consultant Fellow, wishes she had one name. Untidily, she has three: Katie Grant (for everyday), K. M. Grant (for children's and young adult fiction), and now Katherine Grant, the name under which her latest novel, *Sedition*, is published.

Angling for a Bit of Peace

DAVID BEANLAND

The word 'essay' reminds me of school, homework and exams, and induces a mild shudder of dislike. Dr Johnson defined the essay as an irregular, undigested piece, which is probably what my early compositions were, and Ben Jonson thought essayists produced 'a few loose sentences, and that's all'. Yet, as Hazlitt and Lamb proved, essays have been popular when skilfully written, and they still exist in the form of magazine and newspaper articles.

Arthur Ransome was a great admirer of Hazlitt and hankered after producing a series of essays himself. He would probably have considered that his journalism got in the way of that ambition, but in *Rod & Line* he realized it. The book comprises fifty essays distilled from articles he wrote for the *Manchester Guardian* after having complained to the editor that the newspaper 'was not doing what it might for fishermen'. That might put off those readers who are not among the four million anglers in Britain. It shouldn't. Ransome was not a narrow-minded devotee of fly, float and lure but a man of wide interests and experience.

The book was published in 1929 when he was in his early forties. By that time he had had a varied career in publishing and journalism. He had reported from Russia and Egypt, mingled with the Bolsheviks, been divorced and remarried, to Trotsky's secretary. Consequently these pieces are the musings of a mature writer who views angling and other matters with a self-deprecating irony, a detachment infused with humour, and a good dose of wisdom. The pressure of writing a

We can try to obtain second-hand copies of Arthur Ransome, *Rod & Line* (1929).

weekly article probably led Ransome to range more widely than others might have done. Inevitably there is some reference to technicalities, but if an essay on 'Wet Flies for Down-stream Fishing' has no appeal, turn to 'Bulls and Kindred Phenomena', the effect of an eclipse, or a piece on fishing inns.

Virginia Woolf believed that a good essay drew a curtain round the reader, keeping one in, not out. That cosy, comforting feeling is always present in Ransome's essays. He has that knack of addressing you as a friend, a confidant. Nonetheless, authoritative statements do appear, often at the beginning of the essay. 'On Tackle-shops' opens with 'The pleasures of fishing are chiefly to be found in rivers, lakes and tackle-shops and, of the three, the last are the least affected by the weather.' Actually, he was not very interested in lakes, regarding still-water fishing as 'derogatory to human dignity – like betting on horses you have never seen, or marriage in those countries where women are invisible until they are wed'.

Agnes Miller Parker

Angling is a peaceful pursuit, reflected in Isaak Walton's motto 'Study to be quiet', and in this book the easy, clear prose produces a curtained calm. Humour slides in without ruffling the surface. Writing about beginners, Ransome says, 'I fished a little while ago with a man, not in his first youth, who had wasted the flower of his life on business and golf and gardening and motoring and marriage, and had in this way postponed his initiation far too long.'

There's a touching photograph of Arthur and his second wife Evgenia fishing near Riga, the two of them standing side by side, their rods poking hopefully over the water. It's typical that he did not consider himself to be an exceptional angler or a skilled writer. His accomplishments were hard won and made him modest rather than proud. In the essay on 'Fishing in Books and Fishing in Fact' he mocks those writers who angle in Arcadia rather than in real life. His experiences as a hack writer, disappointed husband, struggling author and respected journalist made him acknowledge his failings and so endear himself to the reader.

Unlike the belated beginner, Ransome was introduced to fishing when he was young. His father Cyril was a keen angler as well as a professor of history, but he died when Arthur was 13. Returning from the river in the dark, Cyril tripped and damaged his ankle. There were complications and eventually his leg was amputated, contributing to an early death. Arthur stopped angling then, only taking it up again when in his twenties. We should be grateful that he did. *Rod & Line* is not a full meal, more a delightful hors d'oeuvre, but it is still a dish worth sampling.

DAVID BEANLAND lives in Devon. He contributes to several fishing magazines, writes poetry and carves wood.

Age of Innocence

ANTHONY GARDNER

A while ago I attended a talk by a writer who had grown up in East Germany. What was it like, his audience wanted to know, living in a police state? 'The truth is', he replied, 'that when you're a teenager, politics are much less important than girls and football.'

I thought of this when I rediscovered Godfrey Smith's novel *The Business of Loving* (1961) among my father's old books. Although the core of the story is set during the Second World War, the conflict barely registers beside what is, to the young hero, his raison d'être: the pursuit of an idealized lover. I must have been 16 when I first read it, and nothing I had come across described more perfectly my own state of mind. It clutched at my heart; returning to it in middle age, I found certain phrases and sentences echoing across the years with haunting vividness, like a bell tolling from a submerged city.

The book opens in 1960 with a chance meeting between two childhood friends. Now in their mid-thirties, they haven't seen each other for thirteen years. Felix Weston is a failed writer, while Peregrine 'Benny' Benedict has built up a hugely profitable record company. But Benny's success masks an emotional void. When Benny asks after Laura, a figure from their youth, it becomes clear that the two men represent opposite ends of the romantic spectrum. 'I sometimes wish I could believe in love as he does,' Felix muses to himself; 'because what else is there? Yet what has it brought him but pain and emptiness? And what has not believing in it brought me?'

We can try to obtain second-hand copies of Godfrey Smith, *The Business of Loving* (1961).

The story then moves back to the summer of 1939. Benny and Felix are about to leave Valhalla, their Hampshire prep school, and to the dreamy, academically promising Benny life has never been sweeter: he is brimming with a new-found passion for jazz, and thrills his kindly father – a widowed rep for the Margrave Brewery – by scoring fifty in his final cricket match. Above all, he is in thrall to the idea of love, and as he cycles past the grammar school to which he is about to move, he catches sight of two people who will dominate his adolescence:

> They were a boy and a girl: the boy was about sixteen, the girl looked a little less . . . they sped down the hill and the boy said something which made the girl laugh. Then they were gone.
>
> Benedict cycled on, but he was in a trance. He had never seen anything so – perfect . . . *They must be in love*, he thought. How could any other emotion between them be possible? Benedict tingled with pure, unentangled happiness.

The boy turns out to be the school's brightest star, Tony Hammond – a sportsman, scholar and musician for whom anything seems possible. The girl is Laura Mackay, daughter of the local doctor, and though she appears inseparable from Hammond, Benny falls instantly in love with her. Such is his obsession that he throws away his chances of a scholarship to another school by writing a two-sentence answer to an exam question: 'The poet is right. There is only love.'

Benny is just level-headed enough to realize that Laura is out of his reach – for now at least – and as his teens progress he turns to three other girls for guidance in the ways of women. There is his friend Milo's sweet, timid sister Tessa; his formidably bright classmate Constance, who teaches him how to dance and gives him his first kiss; and, above all, Felix's absurdly young stepmother Arabella, a 19-year-old former artist's model who mesmerizes the boys with her revelations about what women find attractive. But though Benny tells Tessa, 'I'll have to find another girl one day, a real flesh-and-blood one, not a dream girl,' his devotion to Laura and his belief in romance are unwavering.

Then, on the eve of Benny's seventeenth birthday, something extraordinary happens – Tony Hammond disappears in the wake of a mysterious scandal. Laura is now approachable and, to Benny's wonderment, comes to reciprocate his feelings. But the war finally catches up with them: Benny joins the RAF and is sent overseas. As the date of his return approaches, a growing note of panic in Laura's letters makes it clear to the reader – though not to Benny – that things are about to go terribly wrong. The pages describing the collapse of his world are ones that I can still hardly bring myself to read. As the 1960s strand of the narrative makes clear, the shock has never left him: the question is whether his reunion with Felix can help him finally put it behind him.

If there is a more heartfelt prose account of adolescent longing – from the male perspective at least – I can't think of it. Though Benny's friends never tire of telling him how ridiculous his belief in love and honour is, to anyone who shares his romantic disposition he is a hugely sympathetic figure; and part of *The Business of Loving*'s appeal is that the 1940s world it portrays is imbued – despite the war – with an innocence which mirrors Benny's own. The fictional Cressbrook valley in which he grows up is a kind of Eden ('the little hills of the Hampshire Downs cupped it so gently that it was impossible to see the hard-limned horizon. The most distant woods lay in a haze of purple turning lime under the declining sun . . .'); Benny's father inhabits the idealized England beloved of John Major, with its warm beer and long shadows on cricket grounds. The book, indeed, brims with nostalgia: its most characteristic phrase is 'he would always remember'. And yet as a teenager I hardly noticed this beside the freshness and immediacy of its emotional landscape.

Godfrey Smith thought of his book as a riposte to the Angry Young Men of the late 1950s: the bright yellow cover of the Victor Gollancz first edition proclaims it as 'a contemporary novel by a novelist who is very far from being "angry"'. For the young Benny, life is the greatest gift imaginable, and the world is divided into those who affirm and those who deny it; the 'angries' are miserablists who don't realize how lucky they are. I prefer, however, to see *The Business of Loving* in the context of what came after: the rock 'n' roll-fuelled teenage revolution of the 1960s. It is possibly the last novel about adolescence to be blissfully free of the rebellious discontent which has come to be known as 'attitude'.

This is not to say that Benny and his close circle of friends are wedded to the Establishment – far from it. Benny's friend Ken Heppel is a pacifist and chooses to work in the mines rather than fight in the war, while Tony Hammond professes Marxism. But these are intellectual positions that their elders respect or even share (Felix's father is a wealthy communist): there is no sense of 'them' and 'us'. Instead of complaining that they are misunderstood, the teenagers knuckle down to their studies, in the hope of reaching a good university and bettering themselves and the world.

It is the young Benny's intoxication with being alive that makes him such an appealing hero. Even when his love for Laura seems hopeless, he doesn't mope, but manages to see her relationship with Hammond as a splendid thing. What gives the novel a particular edge is that the overwhelming vitality which propels Benny is something much more ambiguous in Hammond, 'like a marvellous and powerful engine with the controls all set in reverse', threatening him with self-destruction.

Education is another theme of the book, and the headmaster of Valhalla, Mr Varley, deserves a place in the pantheon of great comic schoolteachers. A military man of uncertain qualifications, his eccentricity finds full expression in a unique morning service with mimed prayers:

'Help all doctors and nurses,' Mr Varley continued, his eyes tight shut. 'And guide the surgeon's knife.'

A mighty crash shook the room as a hundred small hands came down on the desks in front of them. With the expertise of long practice, the hundred fists slid down the desk lids, performing an imaginary incision with a scalpel.

'Bless all cashiers' – the boys doled out imaginary notes across a putative counter – 'with their special temptations. Bless all sailors and those in peril on the sea' – the boys paid out imaginary anchors . . .

At the end of the novel, Ken Heppel passes judgement on Benny's romanticism: 'We live in the age of the picaresque hero and the positive philosopher; we must do without our illusions. There's no magic in the world except what we put in it.' But while Benny seems to come to terms with his lost love, Godfrey Smith leaves the door open just wide enough to suggest that emotions which run so deep can never be entirely sublimated.

I have always assumed *The Business of Loving* to be heavily auto-biographical. Godfrey Smith went on to write two more novels but then abandoned fiction in favour of journalism. Now almost 90, he still occasionally writes newspaper articles, and when I see them I can't help wondering how much of Benny lives on in him – and in me.

As a teenager, ANTHONY GARDNER papered his room with covers from the *Sunday Times Magazine*, which Godfrey Smith edited. His second novel, *Fox* – a satire on the surveillance society featuring Chinese spies and urban foxes – has recently been published.

A Song of the Islands

PAMELA BEASANT

An Orkney Tapestry sits quietly at the heart of George Mackay Brown's prolific output as a writer of poetry, stories, novels and plays, created over a life that was longer and richer than he or anyone else expected. (Following a diagnosis of TB as a young man, before the introduction of penicillin, he must have felt he was living on borrowed time for almost all his adult life.) For those who have never read him, this small book about his native Orkney serves as a wonderful introduction. For those who have already fallen under his spell, it is something they return to and quote from, and love like an old friend.

My copy is tatty, well-thumbed and browning, and full of torn strips of paper marking certain passages. With its drawings by GMB's friend the Orkney artist Sylvia Wishart, the book has an evocative magic; just to hold it conjures up George and his Orkney, more than anything else he wrote. Somehow, Orkney and George are fused, and while Stromness, his home town, seems to have absorbed him in its stone walls, piers and crow-steps, his absence is still noticeable, a gap in the town, which has changed over the years but also stayed essentially the same. Last year it was twenty years since he died, but I still miss him. (My first ten years in Stromness overlapped with George's last, during which we had a quiet but strong bond to do with poetry, shy on my part.) Picking up *An Orkney Tapestry* is like hearing his voice again.

It's a hard book to sum up because it's a bit of a mishmash of

---

We can try to obtain second-hand copies of George Mackay Brown, *An Orkney Tapestry* (1969).

Sylvia Wishart, 'Stromness'

history, description, essay, poetry and even a short play. It shouldn't hold together at all, but it does, wonderfully, and in fact the pure essence of GMB as a writer is here, set down in his characteristically distilled, poetic prose. The book started out as a commission, and the assumption is that the publishers had in mind a kind of contemporary guidebook to the islands as seen through his eyes. But that kind of writing, involving facts, figures, lists and much tedious research, was not to his taste, and he turned the commission into an opportunity to encapsulate all that was precious and rich about the land and the people of Orkney, in the face of dubious progress, the pernicious influence of television, and the uniformity of thought and opinion imposed by the mass media.

For GMB, everything had a context or a ghost: words, thoughts, stories and people; and everyone in the islands was woven together with a shared history and 'fable' (or vision) of themselves, based on the past, which is everywhere evident. He wanted Orkney people to understand and be proud of this fable, and to define their uniqueness in the context of a kind of woven garment of history.

GMB was born in 1921, and he wrote *An Orkney Tapestry* in his late forties when, after a long, slow start, he was truly finding his voice as a writer and his place as a fully fledged and independent person. At the time of writing his mother had recently died, and he had moved into his own council flat in Stromness; he had emerged

Sylvia Wishart, 'The *Ross Puma* ashore in Hoy'

from some years of heavy drinking verging on alcoholism; he was gaining recognition as a poet and short-story writer; and he was firmly back in his home town, after his only spell away from Orkney at Newbattle Abbey College and Edinburgh University.

Not only that: after the failure of his brief engagement to Stella Cartwright, the 'muse' of many of the Edinburgh poets, he was accepting (not unhappily) that he was destined to remain single, live alone and dedicate himself to writing. Also, significantly, he had converted to Catholicism, rejecting his Presbyterian upbringing; a bold and unusual step in Orkney. He had found himself, and his voice, and in some ways *An Orkney Tapestry* is his manifesto as a writer, and all his creative and spiritual preoccupations and inspirations can be found in this book: the Sagas, the lives of St Magnus and St Rognvald, the Christ figure, the ordinary people, the land, the sea, the drunks and outsiders, and the communities which are sources of strength, resilience and continuity, as well as judgement and narrow-mindedness.

Apart from anything else, the book also contains his most captivating description of the Orkney landscape and weather:

A city shower is a meaningless nuisance, a liquidity seeping into collar and trouser-leg. In the north, on a showery day, you can see the rain, its lovely behaviour over an island – while you stand a mile off in a patch of sun – Jock's cows in the meadow a huddle of ghosts, Tammy's oat field jewelled; the clouds a rout

of fabulous creatures dissolving at last through their prism . . .
Nothing is more lovely than the islands in a shifting dapple of
sun and rain.

There's a whole chapter on Rackwick, in North Hoy; one of the
most beautiful and rarefied places in Orkney, which GMB loved and
often visited. For him, the beauty of the place was underscored by the
harshness of the lives of the people who had eked a meagre living
from the land and dangerous sea. The valley was gradually depopu-
lated until the only farmer left there, Jack Rendall, married, and the
first child born in Rackwick for many years, Lucy, arrived in 1980 – a
joyful, hopeful event, celebrated in GMB's acrostic poem 'Lullaby for
Lucy', and later set to music by Peter Maxwell Davies.

Published in 1969, *An Orkney Tapestry* was still fresh and new
when Peter Maxwell Davies (Max) came on holiday to Orkney in
1970. He bought the book in Stromness, stayed up all night reading
it and, by one of those strange coincidences, met George the following day in Hoy and first set eyes on Bunertoon, a ruined cottage high
up on the cliff at Rackwick, which would become his home for the
next thirty years. GMB's poetry inspired some beautiful new music,
not least the opera *The Martyrdom of St Magnus*, which opened the
first St Magnus Festival in 1977. From that chance meeting, based on
Max's enthusiasm for *An Orkney Tapestry*, so much grew.

And yet *An Orkney Tapestry* remains out of print, at GMB's own
request. It's to be found fairly easily second-hand, but it's an intriguing
and troubling thought that GMB himself was not happy with the
book. He was characteristically tight-lipped about the reasons for this.
Perhaps he felt it was a bit of a jumble of thoughts and ideas. Perhaps
the very things that people love about it did not please him (he was a
severe self-critic). It was certainly longer than anything he had written
before, and his under-confidence about his ability to sustain a long
piece of prose, expressed when his publisher suggested a novel, might
be based on a sense of failure to make a coherent whole of *An Orkney*

Tapestry. And yet, very soon after, he went on to write the wonderful *Greenvoe*, followed by a string of others, culminating in *Beside the Ocean of Time*, shortlisted for the Booker Prize in 1994.

For me, everything GMB wrote came from a deep well of poetry, and a poet's sensibility informs the beauty and distillation of his prose. He is sometimes portrayed as a diffident, even naïve writer, which might be true in some sense; but he knew what he was trying to achieve, and he knew he was good. Far from being some sort of 'mystic sage', he was funny, occasionally mischievous, and very interested in the doings of the town. He worked with great discipline through illness and bouts of depression, and was a generous, perceptive mentor to younger writers.

From his flat in Stromness, he roved through time and space, and channelled his single-minded vision into a body of work that speaks universally. And in the lovely conglomeration of *An Orkney Tapestry* he wove a portrait, a fable for Orkney, whose ongoing threads are deeply rooted here in the islands, but encompass everyone.

PAMELA BEASANT lives in Stromness, Orkney. She is a poet, playwright and non-fiction writer, and has been director of the Orkney Writers' Course for the St Magnus Festival since 2011.

Time Out of War

JEREMY LEWIS

Every now and then a book is so badly published that it never quite recovers, however eloquent its admirers. Robert Kee's account of the three years he spent in a German prisoner-of-war camp is one of the great books of the Second World War; it is also sadly neglected, thanks to the part played in its publication by the novelist Graham Greene.

Greene left MI6 in 1944, and took up a job as the editorial director of Eyre & Spottiswoode, a rather grand, old-fashioned firm of publishers with a strong line in Catholic books. Robert Kee was demobbed from the RAF in 1945, and the following year he sent Greene the typescript of *A Crowd Is Not Company*. No doubt Greene both liked and admired his new acquisition, but he made two fatal publishing errors: he allowed Kee to retain the book's eminently forgettable title, a quotation from Francis Bacon; and, less forgivably, he insisted on publishing what was self-evidently a memoir as a novel, on the grounds that after the First World War it had taken a good ten years before autobiographical accounts of the war – Graves's *Goodbye to All That*, Blunden's *Undertones of War*, Sassoon's *Memoirs of an Infantry Officer* – began to enjoy commercial and literary success.

As it turned out, prisoner-of-war memoirs like *The Wooden Horse*, *The Great Escape* and *The Colditz Story* became bestsellers not long after the publication of *A Crowd Is Not Company* in 1947. Kee had ambitions to become a novelist, and happily went along with Greene's suggestion, but when shortly after publication Peter Quennell told

We can try to obtain second-hand copies of Robert Kee, *A Crowd Is Not Company* (1947).

81

him he couldn't understand why he had agreed to its being published as a novel, 'I immediately wished I hadn't.' The combination of unmemorable title and miscategorization proved fatal to the book's durability and fame; Jonathan Cape reissued it as a memoir in 1982, but the damage had been done.

A product of Stowe and Magdalen College, Oxford, where he had become amorously involved with A. J. P. Taylor's wife, Kee joined the RAF at the outbreak of war, while still in his early twenties. He flew Hampdens on bombing raids over Germany but was shot down over Holland in 1942, captured and eventually sent to a prisoner-of-war camp in what is now part of Poland. 'For you the war is over,' his German captors insisted time and again: isolated from the world at large, he and his fellow-prisoners picked up what they could about the progress of the war from talkative guards and covert tunings-in to the BBC; 'I heard it all from the same patch of sand, four hundred yards long by a hundred wide, in the middle of a Silesian pine forest.'

Camp life veered between moments of unexpected happiness, claustrophobia and intense frustration.

The smooth-phrased BBC announcer, the amusing don, the self-confident politician, the jargon-perfect critic, the editor of the literary magazine – all are reducible within a few weeks to a bewildered defensive creature with hollow cheeks and desperate eyes whose only cares will be to see that he gets his fair share of the potato ration, that nobody steals his bed boards, and that he exchanges his cigarette ends for food or vice versa at the best possible price . . . some tendencies in human behaviour were encouraged, others repressed, and the results were both pleasant and unpleasant.

The POWs were crammed on to wooden bunks in windswept wooden huts, and the resultant overcrowding was unbearable at times: the fact that 'you could never turn your head without seeing some evidence of their closeness – their clothes or their books or their photographs' – led to rows with even the most congenial inmates, all of whom addressed one another with the obligatory 'old man' or 'old boy'. Music, painting and poetry often had an unexpected appeal, and many people who would normally never have had anything to do with such things were forced by their environment to look into them and found there greater wealth than they had ever known before. An extraordinary range of books was available in the camp library, including the complete novels of Thomas Hardy, Frazer's *The Golden Bough*, and works by John Stuart Mill; Kee tells us that at one time he was reading Houghton's *Life of Keats*, and when they were eventually ordered to abandon the camp he took with him, as easy reading, *Tristram Shandy*.

Dreaming of escape was, for most prisoners, no more than an agreeable fantasy, offering 'almost unlimited scope for invention and strategy, and the personal romanticising in bed at night. It was the schoolboy's dream come true.' Kee reluctantly agreed to take part in an attempt to scale the wire fence with ladders after somehow fusing the perimeter lights, and when it failed 'I went about the camp like a man reprieved while on his way to the chaplain and the hangman.'

Despite his earlier sense of relief, Kee later took part in a rather more successful escape attempt. In classic prisoner-of-war style, a tunnel was bored from inside a lavatory block. It grew narrower and more airless as it neared its destination beyond the wire, rather like a 'bottle of hock', and Kee, clutching his possessions in a briefcase, wondered whether he would ever make it out of the vertical hole at the end, or whether he would be stuck fast, waiting to be picked up by a searchlight or a machine-gun. He eventually squeezed himself out and, equipped with a compass and a home-made map, he and his friend Sammy picked their way along a railway track in the direction of the nearest town, from where they planned to take a train to Berlin.

They looked like a couple of tramps – the sole was peeling off one of Kee's boots, and he was smeared with mud after toppling into a pond – but in this they were no different from many of the forced labourers from all over Europe whom they encountered over the next few days. They took a stopping train to Berlin, reckoning that they were less likely to be challenged by officials demanding to see their crudely forged and increasingly smudged identity papers if they travelled on local trains.

> In Berlin the sun was shining from a blue spring sky. I under-
> stood from the conversation of a man and a woman in our
> carriage that there had been an air raid two nights before. There
> were isolated signs of damage: some houses down by the rail-
> way, a burnt-out church – less on the whole than could have
> been seen from a train passing through London at that time.
> But the effect of morning sunshine on the roofs of a terrorised
> city was much the same and even to us sitting in the train it
> seemed very good to be alive.

Many of the Germans they encountered, both in the camp and on their travels, turned out to be kind and friendly.

For some reason Sammy was convinced that they could meet up with members of the Belgian Resistance in Aachen so, claiming to be foreign workers en route to the Krupp armament factory, they boarded a 'huge stallion of a train' bound for Cologne. Although one knows perfectly well that they'll never make it to the Belgian border, Kee's account of their train ride across Germany is a nail-biting tour de force, which suggests that he might indeed have made it as a nov-elist. Needless to say, they were arrested outside Cologne and shipped back to Silesia. But by now the Russians were advancing from the east; the camp was abandoned, and Kee and his fellow-prisoners were force-marched to the west, joining the great waves of displaced humanity – Germans from Prussia and Poland, slave labourers from all over occupied Europe – fleeing from the Russians or simply trying to make their way home.

Although the war was coming to an end, the book finishes on a disillusioned note. Herded into yet another squalid and barely functioning prisoner-of-war camp, a despairing Kee pulls from his pocket an anthology of verse, which had provided so much consolation during his long captivity. 'Once I had believed that the beauty which it contained could never fail, that it redeemed the whole of life. Now the idea was absurd. I thought of the finest pages in the book, and they were worthless,' he writes. He dropped the book on the ground, and 'it lay there for a moment, its leaves turning slowly in the wind which blew over the mud, the breath of a new day. Then it was trampled out of sight by the boots of the man behind me.'

Robert Kee went on to become a publisher, a journalist, a historian and a television reporter and interviewer, famed for his saturnine good looks, but *A Crowd Is Not Company* remains his finest achievement.

JEREMY LEWIS is the deputy editor of *The Oldie*. His biography of David Astor of the *Observer* was published last year.

Along the Old Ways

URSULA BUCHAN

I spend a couple of weeks each year walking on the Lake District fells, so it is inevitable that I should have fallen upon James Rebanks's remarkable *The Shepherd's Life* (2015). I loved it, and I learned much more about upland sheep farming than I could possibly have divined from hours of watching Herdwicks on the fell. Reading *The Shepherd's Life* inevitably set me thinking about another book I read long ago and which, tellingly, turned the young Rebanks into a reader: 'One day, I pulled *A Shepherd's Life* by W. H. Hudson from the bookcase . . . It was going to be lousy and patronizing, I just knew it. I was going to hate it like the books they'd pushed at us in school. But I was wrong, I didn't hate it. I loved it.'

The use of the indefinite article in Hudson's title points to an important difference between the two books, however. Hudson was less interested in conveying the practicalities of shepherding and sheep-breeding than in recording the lives of shepherds. His is a much gentler and more episodic book than Rebanks's but, nevertheless, it's one I've never forgotten.

Readers of *Slightly Foxed* will have noticed quite a strong bias towards writers of well-written pastoral non-fiction, such as Adrian Bell, Ronald Blythe, Richard Hillyer and Richard Mabey. This is scarcely surprising since in this country we seem to have a predilection

---

W. H. Hudson, *A Shepherd's Life: Impressions of the South Wiltshire Downs* (1910)
Sigma Press · Pb · 290pp · £8.99 · ISBN 9780941936859
James Rebanks, *The Shepherd's Life: A Tale of the Lake District* (2015)
Penguin · Pb · 320pp · £9.99 · ISBN 9781041979366

for reading about our countryside and the people who live in it. This preoccupation goes back at least to the time of the Romantic poets and William Cobbett, when burgeoning towns and cities seemed to be eating up the countryside, but it was promoted by the quickening pace of life at the beginning of the twentieth century, when educated people began to see that the valued 'old ways' were threatened, especially by the motor-car. It was at this point that William Henry Hudson, an extremely accomplished field naturalist, began visiting Wiltshire and the surrounding counties and getting to know country dwellers and the wildlife that co-existed with them.

Strangely, Hudson was not bred in England. His Devonian grand-father had settled in New England, but his parents decided to try their luck as sheep-farmers in Argentina, not far from Buenos Aires, and that was where Hudson was born in 1841. His father was declared bankrupt at least once, so they moved around and times were apparently often hard. Hudson seems to have spent a great deal of his childhood out of doors, minutely observing the natural world, and by the time he moved to London in 1874 he was already an expert on South American birds.

In London he married his much older landlady, who ran a couple of boarding-houses, but she too became bankrupt, so the hard times continued. It was a number of years before Hudson was recognized as a writer: for novels such as *Green Mansions*, books on the natural history of both Britain and Argentina, and memoirs of his early life – *Long Ago and Far Away*, *The Naturalist in La Plata* and *Idle in Patagonia*. He wrote a couple of dozen books in all. He was also one of the first chairmen of the Royal Society for the Protection of Birds.

Along the way, he acquired influential literary friends, among them George Gissing and Sir Edward Grey (the greatest ornithologist ever to have been Foreign Secretary) who in 1901 lobbied successfully to get Hudson a pension. Thereafter he could more easily afford to travel, choosing particularly the West Country, moving about on foot or bicycle, and crucially getting away from the city, which he loathed. The result of these wanderings were books of natural history, including *Afoot in England, Birds in Town and Village, Hampshire Days, Nature in Downland* and, his most famous, *A Shepherd's Life*, subtitled *Impressions of the South Wiltshire Downs*.

Howard Phipps, 'Noonday shade', wood engraving

Hudson, bred to the pampas with its almost endless horizons, seems to have been particularly taken by Salisbury Plain, or at least the downland on the southern border of it, which had not been colonized by the Army. In *A Shepherd's Life* he describes lovingly the chalk downs, the green and wooded valleys, and the clear streams of the Wylye, the Avon and the Nadder. The central figure in this landscape is a picturesque old man called Caleb Bawcombe, the pseudonym Hudson chose for a retired head shepherd from a hilltop village he calls Winterbourne Bishop – in fact, Martin on the Hampshire/Wiltshire border. Over a period of time, Hudson got to know Caleb well and heard tales of shepherds and shepherding stretching as far back as 1830.

Hudson's tone is often elegiac: the great bustard was already extinct, and animals and birds, as well as the country folk, were now barred from many woods by Edwardian landowners determined to preserve their pheasant shoots. Hudson rarely has a good word to say about them or their tenants since, as far as he is concerned, they were both exploiters of the landless labourer. He is also vitriolic about Victorian judges who hanged or deported poachers and sheep-stealers and those members of the starving peasantry who were caught breaking up threshing machines.

His choice of a hill shepherd to tell tales of the countryside is not surprising. Shepherds get the most favourable press in the Bible, and ever afterwards have been admired for their sagacity, strength of character and practical expertise – the result of using their sharp eyes on long, lonely vigils. Hudson certainly believed there was a very particular wisdom in shepherds, whom he plainly considered the aristocracy of agricultural labourers: they might earn no more than seven shillings a week, but they were entrusted with valuable stock by their employers and left alone to get on with it. And he admired their inevitably close partnership with that most intelligent of dogs, the Border Collie sheepdog, which can only work well for a master who has considerable patience and understanding.

I was at first struck by Caleb's appearance, and later by the expression of his eyes. A very tall, big-boned, lean, round-shoul-dered man, he was uncouth almost to the point of grotesqueness . . . The hazel eyes were wonderfully clear, but that quality was less remarkable than the unhuman intelligence in them – fawn-like eyes that gazed steadily at you as one may gaze through the window, open back and front, of a house at the landscape beyond.

The book is not all about this shepherd. Hudson also got to know a number of gipsies, whom he liked and admired for their knowledge of natural things, as well as their contempt for a settled life, but about whose attitudes to other people's property he had few illusions.

Hudson was fascinated by what were once called 'old characters', people without schooling or who had left school before they were fully formed, and so went their own way, acquiring in time the gnarled and individual personality of an old oak. Unlettered, they often had a particular richness of speech, both in phrase-making and rhythm, since it was their only means of communication. (Hudson marvels at how, though the Bawcombe family are scattered, they never think to write letters to each other.) I lived in Wiltshire for a time in the mid-1970s and worked on Saturdays with a semi-retired gardener, who used to say about our task of pruning the roses: 'We do be going to nip them climbers.' The rhythms of rural Wiltshire speech therefore have an especial appeal for me, and in *A Shepherd's Life* they are fully on display.

To Hudson, what Caleb had found was a land of lost content. Right at the end of the book he reports him as saying: 'I don't say that I want to have my life again, because 'twould be sinful. We must take what is sent. But if 'twas offered me and I was told to choose my work, I'd say, Give me my Wiltsheer Downs again and let me be a shepherd there all my life long.' Though Hudson is chronicling a life of serenity that he contrasts starkly with that lived by those who crowd together in cities, it would not be fair to call him a sentimentalist (even if many of his followers were). He knew how hard and boring and unrewarding manual labour mostly is, but he also saw how it could forge stout-hearted and admirable, if narrow, characters.

Over the forty or so years since I last read *A Shepherd's Life*, it has lost a little of its charm for me. Hudson is not a particularly elegant stylist, and a few of the stories trail off into inconsequentiality. Lovers of wild flora and fauna will find Hudson's *Hampshire Days* (about the New Forest) a more satisfactory read, since it shows how careful and observant a naturalist he was.

Each man kills the thing he loves, and the way of life that Hudson chronicles – very hard, very poor, and sometimes downright cruel, but rich in texture, and with its own rewards – could not survive urban man's hankering after the countryside. As soon as he was prosperous enough to own a motor-car, he invaded that countryside and chased out its poorer, long-established inhabitants. What the commuter did not do, changes in agriculture, especially during two world wars, achieved. Employed upland shepherds have mostly gone, and those who survive do so in part thanks to the taxpayer. At the turn of the last century, they needed a Hudson to tell their story; these days, they tell their own.

URSULA BUCHAN is an enthusiastic but woefully amateur and ignorant field naturalist.

The Book Cure

KEN HAIGH

I wanted to call this 'How Children's Literature Saved My Life', but the simple truth is that my life was never in any real danger. My *imaginative* life, however, was in grave peril. It hovered on the brink. This is the story of how it was resuscitated in the simplest of ways – by reading children's books.

I have degrees in English literature and library science. I have been an English teacher and a librarian. My love of reading has shaped my life. And yet, a few years back, I almost stopped reading. When given the choice between turning on the television and opening a good book, I would invariably reach for the remote control.

How this sad state of affairs came to be is all too easily told, and I don't suppose I am the only sufferer. I'll bet it happens all the time. For you see, my life had simply become too full to read. I was working six days a week, I had three young children to care for, and that left little time for anything else. If I was lucky I was able to read two books a month – in a good month. Often I read only one. Strange as it may seem, the real crisis came when I joined a book club. You can begin to see the problem. If you only have time to read one or two books a month, it becomes irksome to have your choices dictated for you. They were excellent choices – critically acclaimed, prize-winning novels most of them – but they weren't *my* choices. Reading had once been fun; now it was work. I began to resent these books. And so I stopped reading.

But the desire to read never entirely went away. I was handling books all day long in the library, and I found myself making lists of books I would like to read when I had the time. Needless to say, the lists got longer and the books remained unread. Then one day I was rescued from my melancholy by our Children's Librarian. This was at about the same time that the fourth book in the Harry Potter series was due to be released, and J. K. Rowling was scheduled to do the world's largest book reading at the Skydome in Toronto. I asked our Children's Librarian what all the fuss was about.

'You mean to tell me you haven't read *Harry Potter?*' she asked. I had to confess that I was totally ignorant of Harry Potter. I had no idea who he was. Had he written many books, I asked. She rolled her eyes and went to the stacks, where she found *Harry Potter and the Philosopher's Stone.* 'Here,' she said, 'read that.'

I did. I read it that night, after the children had gone to bed, in one long, delirious sitting. I devoured the book. I stayed up much too late and was exhausted the next morning, but I had achieved an epiphany of sorts. I had rediscovered my love of reading.

I had also discovered that the fault wasn't really in me, but in the books I had chosen to read. With so little time to read, I had decided that my reading time could not be wasted on frivolous books. I would only read serious books, modern literary masterpieces. But the truth was these books bored me. I could only take so many consciously literary novels of childhood trauma or family dysfunction or the immigrant experience. I felt bad about it. If I wasn't appreciating what was on offer, then it was obviously my fault, there was something lacking in me.

What I discovered on reading Harry Potter was that many of these acclaimed modern authors had forgotten one of the most basic premises of telling a story – they had forgotten how to tell a story. Literary artifice had gotten in the way of good plotting and character development. I also discovered that I was not alone in this assessment. Philip Pullman once said, in a speech when accepting the 1995 Carnegie Medal for his children's story *The Golden Compass*, that in adult literary fiction 'stories are there on sufferance. Other things are felt to be more important: technique, style, literary knowingness . . .

The present-day would-be George Eliots take up their stories as if with a pair of tongs. They're embarrassed by them. If they could write novels without stories in them, they would. Sometimes they do.'

Hearing this was very reassuring. I devised a plan. I would make reading fun again. I would take a book cure, and I would begin by casting my mind back to my childhood and by rereading those books that I had discovered and loved and that had inspired my love of reading ever since. I began with *The Hobbit* and quickly moved on to *Kim* and *The Jungle Books*. With some difficulty I located copies of Walter R. Brooks's witty Freddy the Pig stories: *Freddy the Detective, Freddy Goes Camping, Freddy Goes to Florida*. These were the first chapter books I had read on my own. They were better than I remembered. I tracked down a copy of Ronald Welch's *The Gauntlet*, a time-travelling fantasy about a boy who finds an old gauntlet which transports him back to the Welsh Borders at the time of the Middle Ages. I read and I read and I read, and a strange thing began to happen: the number of books I read each month began to rise, from two to four to twelve.

I found allies in my book cure. Once I told the Children's Librarian what I was up to, she began to recommend titles that I had never come across before: Philip Pullman's *Dark Materials* trilogy, Neil Gaiman's *Coraline*, L. M. Boston's Green Knowe books, Susan Cooper's *Dark Is Rising* sequence. I began to branch out and try books that I had somehow missed in my childhood: *The Wind in the Willows, Swallows and Amazons* and *The Wouldbegoods*.

My daughter also helped. She had progressed beyond the picture-book stage, and we began reading chapter books together at bedtime. We started with the Little House books, books I'd avoided as a boy because, well, they were for girls. We found them fascinating. We moved on to the Chronicles of Narnia. These were more problematic. While we enjoyed *The Lion, the Witch and the Wardrobe* and *The Horse and His Boy*, we found *The Last Battle* simply baffling. Then we began to read the Harry Potter series together. We could hardly wait each night for the day to end, so we could begin a new chapter. We have now finished Harry Potter and we are debating where to turn next. Should we try *Anne of Green Gables, Elijah of Buxton* or *The Secret Benedict Society*?

Now don't misunderstand me. I am not saying that we should all give up on adult fiction. Children's books exist in a fairly simple moral universe which doesn't always reflect adult reality (although, to be fair, some children's books are surprisingly sophisticated). I have gone back to reading books written for adults, but I am more discriminating now. I want substance over style. I am no longer afraid to give up on a book if I find it dull – even if it *has* won the Booker prize. I expect a good story.

If you are in the same situation as I was, if you have grown weary of reading, try my book cure. What were the stories you loved as a child, the ones you couldn't bear to finish because they were so good? Track them down. Read them again. You may rediscover your love of reading.

KEN HAIGH is a librarian and the author of *Under the Holy Lake: A Memoir of Eastern Bhutan* (University of Alberta Press).

Bibliography

Brian Bates, *The Way of an Actor*   35

George Mackay Brown, *An Orkney Tapestry*   76

William Cowper, *The Centenary Letters*   29

Christopher Ricks and Jim McCue (eds.), *The Poems of T. S. Eliot*   51

W. H. Hudson, *A Shepherd's Life*   86

Robert Kee, *A Crowd Is Not Company*   81

John le Carré, *Tinker, Tailor, Soldier, Spy*   7

John McGahern, *The Barracks*   41

Hilary Mantel, *Giving up the Ghost*   13

Maps: in books   55

Noël Mostert, *Frontiers: The Epic of South Africa's Creation and the
    Tragedy of the Xhosa People*   46

Violet Needham, *The Black Riders*   63

Arthur Ransome, *Rod & Line*   68

Reading: rediscovering one's love of   91

Godfrey Smith, *The Business of Loving*   71

Albert Payson Terhune, *Lad: A Dog*   25

Leo Tolstoy, *War and Peace*   18

The *Slightly Foxed* Crossword No. 8: Answers

Across: 1 IN WHAT HOUR 6 RQMS 10 ACTON 11, 17 SIEGFRIED SASSOON
12 HELSTONE 13 EPPIE 15 SAINTLY 19 ALGERIA 22 WOLFE 24 LARK
RISE 27 LAMPEDUSA 28 SCOOP 29 ETNA 30 SANDCASTLE

Down 1,16 IVAN TURGENEV 2, 21 *across* WUTHERING HEIGHTS 3 AGNES
4 HISTORY 5 USELESS 7 QUILP 8 SUDDENNESS 9 AFTER SKI
14 OSCAR WILDE 18 OF HIS SORT 20 AGLAURA 21 HARLAND 23
LOMAN 25 RASTA 26 EPEE

Blowing Our Own Trumpet!

'*Slightly Foxed* has burrowed itself into my consciousness and become essential. One day I may be able to do the crossword, but I'm not holding my breath. Thank you for the most utterly charming periodical in the English-speaking world.'
R. Kuin, France

'I can't imagine facing our election season without *SF* and its power to calm, enlighten and delight. Thank you for your swift action (and, of course, for your existence).'
C. Strug, USA

'I actually discovered *Slightly Foxed* via one of your postcards sent to me from very old dear friends, extolling your virtues, and started a subscription forthwith. I have never regretted it!'
E. Lyngaas, Edinburgh

COMING ATTRACTIONS

YSENDA MAXTONE GRAHAM hears the news from Tartary · MICHAEL BARBER recites from *The Dragon Book of Verse* · MELISSA HARRISON revisits *Frost in May* · MICHAEL HOLROYD celebrates John Stewart Collis · SUE GEE gets lost in translation · ANDREW MERRILLS meets Flavia de Luce · MAGGIE FERGUSSON interviews Ali Smith · JOHN KEAY captures the scorpion-fish · PENELOPE LIVELY sets sail for Tasmania